# BBC QUIZBOOKS
# MASTERTEAM

# Masterteam

compiled by
Rosalind Gold

with a foreword by
Angela Rippon

BBC BOOKS

Published by BBC Books
A division of BBC Enterprises Ltd
Woodlands, 80 Wood Lane, London W12 0TT

First published 1987
Reprinted 1987

ISBN 0 563 20600 4

Photoset by Wilmaset
Birkenhead, Wirral

Printed in Great Britain by
Richard Clay Ltd, Bungay, Suffolk

# CONTENTS

# FOREWORD

Let me tell you, being the host of a regular quiz programme like *Masterteam* is a very humbling experience.
You see, I'd always reckoned that I was of pretty average
intelligence. Not exactly Brain of Britain material admit-
tedly, but not a dumb bell either. And then I started
working on *Masterteam*.

It's not just that our contestants seem to know about
anything from Anthrax to Zen Buddhism, but that they can
deliver their answers so quickly. Like most people, if I
could be given ten seconds or so to dig around in the files
of my memory banks, I could probably come up with an
answer to most things. But it's the skill of instant recall –
that confident way of rattling off the answer with all the
assurance of knowing that it couldn't possibly be anything
else – that leaves me, and the rest of the production team,
open-mouthed with admiration.

It is also the thing that hooks the viewers. I've lost count
of the number of taxi drivers, women in supermarkets, or
people met at parties, who buttonhole me to voice their
admiration for 'that bloke who knew his pop music' or 'that
fellow who was so good on sport', or the woman who 'had
all the answers in the general knowledge'.

Because all of our contestants are ordinary folk, like you
and me, and not high-flying academics or university
professors, we can all identify with them, while at the same
time recognising that extra something that sorts the
winners from the 'also rans'.

But having the answers is only half of the story. The
biggest hurdle for most of our contestants is getting over
the nerves and butterflies, and sometimes even the sheer
terror of being on television. Knowing that every move you
make, every answer you give, right or wrong, is going to be
seen by anything up to eight million people can have a
devastating effect on the equilibrium. The stomach feels
sick, the mouth goes dry and, worst of all, the mind goes
blank. To make our teams feel more confident and
comfortable in the studio, we organise our recording days
so that everyone gets a full rehearsal during the day. It
gives them the opportunity to familiarise themselves with

the layout of their desks, the rules of the game, the use of the buzzers, and the speed of the questions. That's the thing that many players find difficult to grasp on their first run.

In any quiz game, and even in the highly popular quiz leagues run by pubs and social clubs around the country, you have time to think about an answer. But in our game the whole essence of the programme is that you should get in as many questions and answers as possible within a timed section. So obviously the faster I can ask the questions and the quicker you can get the answers, the more points you are likely to score. As one regular viewer noted 'You don't hang around on *Masterteam*.'

We record the series at weekends. Two programmes on a Saturday, and three on Sunday. Because the show runs for five days a week it obviously would not be possible to say to contestants 'Join us on Monday, but if you hit a winning streak you might still be with us on Thursday'. After all, people have jobs to go to! So the weekend routine means that in two days we can put a whole week's programming in the can – though it does make for a hectic schedule. I start at just after 9.30 a.m. on Saturday morning, when I meet up at the studio with Rosalind Gold, our associate producer, and her assistant. Together we go through all the questions that could be asked in that day's programmes. That means four sets of general knowledge questions for the team rounds and twenty-four groups of specialist questions for the Spotlight rounds. I do this to familiarise myself with any awkward or foreign names, as it would be terribly unfair to mislead someone because of bad pronunciation. It also gives us a chance to hear what the questions sound like when read out loud. That may sound elementary, but occasionally something that looks perfectly clear when written down can take on a slightly different emphasis when read out, simply because the contestants can't see the punctuation or structure of the sentence. So we make sure that in presenting the question we leave the contestant in no doubt about what he or she is being asked. We also check for ambiguity and try to ensure that the answer we are looking for is a definite statement of fact. If there are too many grey areas, or possible interpretations, then we discard the question.

Occasionally I get answers from contestants that just might be correct, but need a second opinion. On these occasions we have to stop the recording to check the interpretation. Frankly I hate doing this because it always breaks the contestants' concentration and sometimes it can take a while for them to get back into their stride. So we try to keep our questions and answers as unambiguous as possible.

On Sunday morning I repeat the process with the questions for that day's recordings. It means that I get through about a thousand questions and answers in two days. People often ask me if I remember them all, but I have to admit that I don't. Some of the facts stick for ever (don't ask me why, but I'll always remember now that Torquemada was the leader of the Spanish Inquisition, and that Lemmy is the lead singer with the pop group Motorhead), but most of the facts just pass through into oblivion, simply because of the speed at which I ask the questions. And, after all, I'm the one who has everything written down in front of me, so I don't have to remember, do I?

At the end of each day's recording we entertain our contestants to some of the BBC's famous hospitality (or hostility as it is affectionately known!). That's when they really do relax. With the winners wearing their medals — bronze for two consecutive wins, silver for three and gold for four. There is always a little agonising over questions they got wrong and should have known the answers to, but mostly there is nothing but friendship and camaraderie — losing teams wish the gold medal winners luck in the semi-finals, and often teams from neighbouring parts of the country forge friendships and challenge each other to quiz matches in their local pubs and clubs. I always feel it's a great credit to the teams you never see — the production teams who prepare the questions and look after the contestants — that so many of our players say that, win or lose, they had a 'smashing day out'. Lots of our lady contestants especially say how much they enjoyed the pampering of make-up and hair-dressing, and having their outfits pressed and looked after by wardrobe. And all our teams praise the way they are looked after and cosseted by their production 'minders'. It all helps to make

*Masterteam* one of the happiest programmes I have ever worked on.

There is of course a serious side to the whole thing. There is a trophy to be won at the end of nine weeks, and some of our contestants take the whole thing very seriously indeed. It's strange, don't you think, that with so many quiz and games shows on television, the bigger the prize, the easier the questions seem to be, the smaller the prize, the harder the questions and the greater the distinction of winning. After all, our 'medals' and books or record tokens, and the *Masterteam* trophy and tankards for the winning finalists, hardly compare with the holidays for two in the Bahamas offered on some programmes. But the prestige of winning is obviously important. And long may it continue.

As the host of the show I get to work with a great bunch of people, in front of and behind the cameras, both contestants and production staff. Reading this book, with its thousands of questions from the past two series, should give you some idea of what it's like to be a *Masterteam* contestant, and watching the programme can fill in some of the gaps. But perhaps, more than that, it will whet your appetite and persuade you to form a team of your own. In which case, why not join us, we'd love to have you along? In the meantime, you're no doubt anxious to pit your wits against our questioners. So – let's play; your time starts – now.

*Angela Rippon*

# A NOTE BEFORE PLAYING

On television, *Masterteam* is played by two competing teams of three people. Each game begins with a round of quick-fire general knowledge questions called 'team challenge' when the teams race for their buzzers to answer. At the end of 'team challenge', the team with the higher score chooses a member of the opposing team to go under the 'spotlight'. Six subjects then appear from which the first victim has to choose one on which to answer questions. During the course of a game four people will go under the 'spotlight' (alternating between the two teams) and four 'spotlight' subjects will be chosen. The game is rounded off with another round of 'team challenge'.

This book is set out so that each game follows the pattern described above. You will find that each game begins and ends with a general knowledge round with six 'spotlight' subjects in between which vary from game to game. If you are playing at home with family or friends you will easily be able to play the game in teams – after all, a team need only consist of one person – and if you are on your own you can challenge yourself to a game!

If you are playing in teams and have a spare person present willing to act as question-master you will have great fun. But you can just as easily dispense with the question-master and have just as much fun asking each other the questions.

You can set a time limit of one minute for each round or you can take all the questions in a round – it's up to you!

The questions in the book were all asked during the first two series of *Masterteam*.

*Rosalind Gold*

# GAME 1

1   Who wrote the futuristic novel *1985*?

2   Which religious ceremony is performed with bell, book and candle?

3   What is the German equivalent of the RAF?

4   Which photographer won Academy Awards for the costumes in *Gigi* and *My Fair Lady*?

5   Which former prime minister was once news editor of *The Church Times* (1948–9)?

6   What was banned on London Underground trains in 1984?

7   Which group of peers ranks next after dukes?

8   Who was the first world heavyweight champion to lose and regain his title?

9   To which ancient singing group did Parthenope belong?

10  Which gas is produced by the Haber-Bosch process?

11  What does the surname Phillips, as in Captain Mark Phillips, mean?

12  What other name is given to the feast of Twelfth Night?

1  In cricket, what kind of ball is a Chinaman?

2  Since 1896, how many times have the Olympic Games been cancelled?

3  Who was the first player to hold both the snooker and billiards world championship titles at the same time?

4  In cricket, what is the name of the crease, or white line, painted 4ft in front of the stumps?

5  In which sport do you find a tin, a service box and a telltale?

6  You have heard the expression 'Gordon Bennett' used, but with which sport is this name connected?

7  Who were the two boxers involved in the so-called Battle of the Long Count in 1927?

8  Which horse won the 1983 Derby?

9  What colour is a beginner's belt in judo?

10  In which sport can you score a 'spare' and a 'strike'?

11  In which event, at the 1972 Olympics, did Mary Peters win a gold medal?

12  The Fastnet race is the last event of which yachting competition?

## FOOD AND DRINK

1   Orange juice and Galliano are two of the three ingredients of a Harvey Wallbanger. What is the third?

2   Raita is a refreshing Indian salad. What is always used as a base?

3   Which Scottish town is renowned for its smokies?

4   The process of heating beer or wine with spices or sugar to make a hot drink is called what?

5   The New Zealand strain of Chinese gooseberry is now known by what other name?

6   If an American recipe tells you to broil a dish, how should you cook it?

7   What is the smallest plant in the onion family?

8   What is the old name (still used at banquets) for a double sirloin of beef joined at the backbone?

9   Why is monosodium glutamate sometimes added to foods?

10  Which soup takes its name from the Tamil word meaning 'pepper water'?

11  What are the two main ingredients of devils on horseback?

12  Which variety of fish is traditionally eaten by Poles on Christmas Eve?

1 What was Wellington's answer when threatened with the revelation of compromising letters?

2 During the First World War, whose face appeared on the poster with the caption: 'Your Country Needs You'?

3 Nelson commanded the fleet, but who was Flag Captain of HMS *Victory* at Trafalgar?

4 Which Anglo-Saxon kingdom was bounded to the west by Offa's Dyke?

5 Which London museum was founded in 1753 and opened to the public in 1759?

6 In 1626, on which island did the Dutch found the township of New Amsterdam?

7 Which Irish leader was murdered after signing the 1921 treaty with Britain which established the Irish Free State?

8 In 1170, who was the victim of the assassins Reginald Fitzurse, William de Tracy, Hugh de Merville and Richard le Breton?

9 What was defended, unsuccessfully, between 22 February and 6 March 1836, by fewer than 200 men under Colonel William Travis?

10 Who lived alone in the Bastille from 1698 until his death in 1703?

11 Which memorable history book contains 103 good things, 5 bad kings and 2 genuine dates?

12 Which phrase described the close relations of Britain and France at the start of this century?

## POP MUSIC

1  Which group held a farewell concert on 28 June 1986 at Wembley?

2  On the Rolling Stones album *Aftermath*, to whom did Mick Jagger pledge himself on bended knee?

3  How many number one hits have The Who had in this country?

4  With which Beatles song did Elton John have an American number one hit?

5  Chuck Berry, to date, has had only one number one British hit. What was it?

6  Who wrote Buddy Holly's posthumous number one hit, *It Doesn't Matter Anymore*?

7  With which Malcolm McLaren-managed band did Boy George once sing?

8  Which group achieved a simultaneous first and second placing in the British singles chart in 1984?

9  Which singer's first hit was *Dumb Blonde*?

10  What is the real name of Lemmy of Motorhead?

11  Which famous actor, noted for his sinister roles in horror films, was the narrator on Michael Jackson's single *Thriller*?

12  What was the name of Billy J. Kramer's backing group?

1  What event, in 1969, prompted President Nixon's comment: 'This is the greatest week in the history of the world since the creation'?

2  Which unforgettable film won the Oscar for best picture in 1965?

3  Which horse won the Cheltenham Gold Cup in three consecutive years during the sixties?

4  Who had the original hit with *Concrete and Clay* in 1965?

5  Who, in a speech in 1961, advised British workers: 'Gentlemen, I think it is about time we pulled our fingers out.'?

6  In 1965, which creature escaped from London Zoo and took up residence in Regent's Park, avoiding recapture for twelve days?

7  Who was the pilot of the American U2 spy plane shot down by the Russians in 1960?

8  When England beat Germany to win the World Cup in 1966, what was the score?

9  In 1966, who was the first Briton to fly solo round the world?

10  In 1966, which national daily newspaper changed its format by putting news on the front page?

11  Which Moroccan town was destroyed by an earthquake in February 1960?

12  In which year was the voting age lowered from twenty-one to eighteen?

1   On which long-running series would you hear the catchphrase: 'Book 'em, Dano'?

2   In which London district is *Only Fools and Horses* set?

3   Which Western centred on the adventures of the Cartwright family?

4   In which year did Channel Four take to the screen?

5   Which dog was made famous by his appearances on *Tiswas* and *OTT*?

6   What instrument is played by Lori Singer in the series *Fame*?

7   Which programme travels round the country inviting people to bring their family heirlooms for examination?

8   What was the name of the bumbling detective portrayed by Peter Falk?

9   Which drama series, based on a novel by Jeffrey Archer, traced the careers of ambitious politicians?

10  Which character in *Last of the Summer Wine* is famous for her wrinkled stockings?

11  What was Ria's husband's profession in *Butterflies*?

12  What is the name of Russ Abbot's secret agent character?

1   What nationality was the man who won the 1986 London marathon?

2   What name is often given to the suspension of organic molecules from which life is thought to have evolved?

3   Who played the hunchback in the 1923 film of *The Hunchback of Notre Dame*?

4   Which British group reached number one in the United States with *Wild Thing*?

5   In Greek mythology, which Titan was compelled to support the sky on his shoulders as punishment for rebelling against Zeus?

6   What was the speciality of the eccentric troupe called Wilson, Keppel and Betty?

7   Up, down and strange are the three types of what in physics?

8   How many people are always present at a witches' coven?

9   Which snake has the same name as an air-to-air missile?

10  What name is given to the turf wall built by the Romans from the Forth to the Clyde?

11  In which play will you hear the words: 'Dead! and . . . never called me mother!'?

12  On 7 May 1915, a passenger liner was sunk by a German submarine off the coast of Ireland. What was her name?

# GAME 2

## GENERAL KNOWLEDGE (1)

1  In 1936, which dictator was shot and wounded in the nose by the Hon. Violet Gibson?

2  In which type of well is water forced to the surface by natural pressure?

3  Orpheus, in mythology, and Lot's wife in the *Old Testament* made the same grievous mistake. What was it?

4  Which fictional character is heir to the Earldom of Dorincourt?

5  Found throughout the human body, what are erythrocytes?

6  In which London thoroughfare is the Royal Albert Hall?

7  In theatrical cosmetics, what is the colloquial name of the colour used for blood?

8  What was the original name of Istanbul?

9  Which 'brothers' form a comic duo comprising Rik Mayall and Ade Edmondson?

10  Who was British Minister of Information in the First World War and Minister of Aircraft Production in the Second?

11  In Robert Burns's poem *Tam O' Shanter* the hero used a legendary method of escaping from witches. What was it?

12  Which property, once called Shangri La, did President Eisenhower rename after his grandson?

1   If you were shopping in the store called Gum in which city would you be?

2   When crossing the international date line, what happens to the date when travelling from west to east?

3   The first shots of the American Civil War were fired at Fort Sumter. In which state is it?

4   In which English county is the Bluebell Line steam railway?

5   Which country's international car registration letters are ZA?

6   What is the capital of Vietnam?

7   What is the name of the southernmost of the old provinces of Spain in which Seville, Granada and Cordoba all lie?

8   Which British island, bought by the National Trust in 1969, issues its own postage stamps featuring puffins?

9   What do we usually call the mountain known to the Arabs as Jebel or Jabal Musa, the Mountain of Moses?

10  In which South American region is Welsh widely spoken?

11  On what river does Lisbon, the capital of Portugal, stand?

12  Is the capital of the Falkland Islands on East or West Falkland?

1 Who shot Liberty Valance?

2 What was the name of Goldfinger's bodyguard in the film of that name?

3 Who played Charlie, Marlon Brando's older brother, in *On the Waterfront*?

4 Which screen monster was discovered on Skull Island?

5 What is the occupation of John Cleese in *Clockwise*?

6 Which American director/choreographer was responsible for spectacular dance routines in films such as *42nd Street*?

7 Which broadway musical, starring Ethel Merman, became a film in 1962, starring Rosalind Russell?

8 Which German shell-shock victim was rescued from a trench in 1918, taken to Los Angeles, and had a highly successful film career until his death in 1932?

9 Who was the portly, long-suffering lady who served as the butt of so many of the Marx Brothers' most cruel jokes?

10 Who led the expedition in *Journey to the Centre of the Earth*?

11 Which British studio was responsible for *Passport to Pimlico* and *The Lavender Hill Mob*?

12 Who directed *The Seventh Seal*, *The Silence* and *Through a Glass Darkly*?

# LIVING WORLD

1   What does a camel store in its hump?

2   Why is the nest of the sociable weaverbird unusual?

3   Which member of the cat family is unable to retract its claws?

4   There are three species of snake native to Britain; adder and grass snake are two. What is the third?

5   To which fish family does the goldfish belong?

6   A quadruped is a four-footed animal. What is a palmiped?

7   Which American mammal is distinguished by its bandit mask across the eyes?

8   Which colourful small bird is capable of flying backwards?

9   How is the whale-headed stork better known?

10  If a plant exhibits phototropism what is it doing?

11  Which insect is affected by Isle of Wight disease?

12  Which Scottish game bird was extinct in Britain for 100 years, but was successfully reintroduced from Sweden in 1837?

# LITERATURE

1   Who lived in a forest under the name of Saunders?

2   For which book did Salman Rushdie win the Booker Prize in 1981?

3   Which of Tom Stoppard's plays is based on two characters from *Hamlet*?

4   In *Les Misérables*, what was Jean Valjean's first crime?

5   In *A Tale of Two Cities* whose life was saved when Sydney Carton took his place on the guillotine?

6   In *The Caine Mutiny* what was the name of the commander against whom the mutiny was directed?

7   Who wrote the words of *Auld Lang Syne*?

8   Who shrieked and squeaked in 'fifty different sharps and flats'?

9   In *The Importance of Being Earnest*, who was originally responsible for losing Jack Worthing when he was a baby?

10  Which novel is sub-titled 'A Romance of Exmoor'?

11  The sight of which of King Arthur's knights tempted the Lady of Shalott away from her mirror and loom?

12  What was the name of the Jew of Malta in the play by Marlowe?

## THE 1970s

1 Who died in 1972, having been a great attraction at London Zoo for many years?

2 Which organisation, founded in 1961 by Peter Benenson, won the Nobel Peace Prize in 1977?

3 The Baader-Meinhof gang was active in Germany during the 1970s: what was the forename of either Baader or Meinhof?

4 Who served as American Secretary of State from 1973 to 1977?

5 Who was named as 'the fourth man' in the Burgess-Maclean-Philby spy scandal and deprived of his knighthood by the Queen in 1979?

6 In which sporting event was Charlotte Brew the first woman to compete in 1977?

7 Which million-seller of the 1970s, by Don McLean, was an account of the decline of rock'n'roll since Buddy Holly's death?

8 In 1971, the editors of which underground magazine were sentenced to imprisonment under the Obscene Publications Act?

9 In 1976 Prince Bernhard of the Netherlands and former Japanese Prime Minister Tanaka were involved in a bribes scandal. What was it?

10 Who succeeded Georges Pompidou as President of France in 1974?

11 What was the name of the super tanker which ran aground off the coast of Brittany in March 1978?

12 What replaced Purchase Tax in 1973?

## CLASSICAL MUSIC

1  Which piece by Handel has been performed at every English Coronation since that of George II?

2  Which of Puccini's heroines is an opera singer?

3  Which of Aaron Copland's ballets is based on the life of an American gun-fighter?

4  What is a leitmotiv?

5  To which symphony was Haydn referring when he said: 'That will make the ladies jump'?

6  *Tritsch-Tratsch*, *Furioso* and *Unter Donner und Blitz* are all what?

7  Which Hungarian composer and pianist took holy orders in 1865?

8  How many dancers perform the dance of the cygnets in *Swan Lake*?

9  By what name is the third movement of Debussy's *Suite Bergamasque* commonly known?

10  Who was the composer husband of the nineteenth-century concert pianist Clara Wieck?

11  Andrew Lloyd Webber's composition, *Variations*, is based on a theme by which composer?

12  In which opera does the servant Leporello sing an aria listing his master's amorous conquests?

1 Which fictional sleuth made his first appearance in *Whose Body?* in 1923?

2 What was John Hancock signing when he said: 'There, I guess King George will be able to read that'?

3 Which great English architect and dramatist was imprisoned in the Bastille on a spying charge by Louis XIV?

4 Which two aircraft carriers sailed with the Falklands task force?

5 Which theatre is the Dublin home of the Irish National Theatre Society?

6 Which army personnel are called Red Caps?

7 Which painter is said to have proved his skill and artistry to the Pope by drawing a perfect circle freehand?

8 What is the distinctive feature of a mansard roof?

9 What is known as the fisherman's ring?

10 To which of his many loves did Zeus appear in the form of a swan?

11 In the game of Scrabble, how many points is the letter X worth?

12 In which year did the National Health Service come into operation?

# GAME 3

1 What was the name of the horse which won the Cheltenham Gold Cup on five consecutive occasions between 1932 and 1936?

2 Which manned spacecraft was the first to orbit the moon in 1968?

3 Which famous spy was shot, on 15 October 1917, at Vincennes near Paris?

4 According to the *Book of Revelation*, on what horse does Death ride?

5 According to Tears for Fears, who wants to rule the world?

6 What did the Norse god Odin sacrifice in order to gain wisdom?

7 How is the prison camp Oflag Four-C more familiarly known?

8 What has been mined in the Northwich region of Cheshire since the late seventeeth century?

9 Superman's father was Jor-el, but what was his mother's name?

10 Who was the last Stuart monarch?

11 Who knitted Cock Robin's shroud?

12 Of which Church are the First Presidency and the Council of the Twelve Apostles the ruling bodies?

# THE 1960s

1  Which British building celebrated its 900th anniversary in 1965?

2  Which satirical magazine first appeared on 25 October 1961?

3  In 1966 which spy, serving a forty-one-year prison sentence, escaped from Wormwood Scrubs?

4  Which award was created in 1965, for achievements in export and technology?

5  Which American pop artist and film-maker was shot, but not killed, in 1968?

6  Which entrepreneur's washing machine empire crashed in 1964?

7  In 1968, which musical was notorious for introducing nudity to London theatre-goers?

8  Which woman doctor walked from John O'Groats to Land's End to demonstrate the benefits of vegetarianism?

9  What was the name of the block of flats which collapsed in London in 1968?

10  Of which Russian ballet company was Rudolf Nureyev a member at the time of his defection in 1961?

11  Who defeated Henry Cooper in the fight for the world heavyweight title in May 1966?

12  Which pop singer had *No Particular Place To Go* in 1964?

1 Which Boston bar does Sam Malone run?

2 Which series was the saga of the Seaton family in the north-east during the Depression?

3 In *Cagney and Lacey* what did Mary Beth Lacey call her baby daughter?

4 In which 1960s soap opera did Ryan O'Neal and Mia Farrow co-star?

5 Who created the popular glove puppet Sooty?

6 On American police shows, when a detective calls for an APB what do the initials stand for?

7 In which series was the central character referred to as Number Six?

8 Who regularly introduces *Grandstand* on BBC 1 on Saturdays and Sundays?

9 In the long-running television series *Face to Face*, who interviewed the distinguished faces?

10 What was the title of the sequel to *Please Sir!*?

11 Which television couple have Barney and Betty Rubble as their neighbours?

12 Who is the constant companion of *Postman Pat*?

1 Which famous contralto worked as a telephone switchboard operator before her rise to fame?

2 Which eccentric French composer wrote *Three Pear-Shaped Pieces* and *Limp Preludes for a Dog*?

3 In 1848, after which Austrian Field-Marshal did Johann Strauss the Elder name a march?

4 Which traditional English tune is mentioned twice in *The Merry Wives of Windsor*?

5 What did Gustav Holst describe Saturn as?

6 In 1926, during the première of which opera by Puccini did the conductor, Toscanini, turn to the audience and say: 'The opera ends here because the composer died at this point'?

7 Which composer was known as the Red Priest because of the colour of his hair?

8 Which ballet, by Stravinsky, caused a riot at its first performance in 1913?

9 On his deathbed, in 1825, the Italian composer Salieri confessed to murdering which of his rivals?

10 Which Gilbert and Sullivan opera is set in the Tower of London?

11 What is the popular name of Chopin's *Prelude No. 15 in D Flat*, Opus 28?

12 Who set to music poems in Latin, Old German and Old French from a medieval manuscript found in a Benedictine monastery?

# SPORT

1 Which English football team plays in the Scottish football league?

2 Who lost a shoe, but won a gold medal, in the 1986 European athletics championships?

3 Who was Aleksandr Zaitsev's most famous ice-skating partner?

4 At which sport would you encounter a rover, a peg and a baulk line?

5 What did the Washington Redskins win in 1983, and the Los Angeles Raiders in 1984?

6 Who rode the ill-fated Shergar to victory in the 1981 Derby?

7 What are the dimensions of a snooker table?

8 At Wimbledon, in 1969, whom did Ricardo Gonzales beat in the longest match ever recorded?

9 Which woman sailed around the world in a yacht single-handed, finishing at Dartmouth in June 1978?

10 How many faults are normally imposed for knocking down a fence in showjumping?

11 Whom did Boris Becker defeat in the 1985 Wimbledon men's singles final?

12 What did Boris Onishenko do that caused a scandal in the 1976 Olympics?

1   What began at St John's, Newfoundland, on 14 June 1919, and ended at Clifden, Ireland, 16 hours and 27 minutes later?

2   Name the ship which first came to the *Titanic*'s assistance when she sank?

3   What is the chief water thoroughfare of Venice?

4   What is the name of the state airline of the Soviet Union?

5   What form of transport is a felucca?

6   Which British train made its final journey on 30 April 1972?

7   The aircraft with the widest ever wingspan was dubbed 'the Spruce Goose'. Which eccentric film producer designed it?

8   What is the derivation of the word 'cab', meaning taxi?

9   Which British motor manufacturer introduced Henry Ford's production methods into Britain?

10  Which of Stephenson's locomotives was used at the opening ceremony of the Stockton to Darlington line?

11  What was the destination of Concorde on its first scheduled flight from Heathrow on 21 January 1976?

12  Who built the first British four-wheeled petrol-driven car?

# HISTORY

1 Who is the only Englishman to have been both knighted and canonised?

2 Which American president introduced Prohibition?

3 How was the Emperor Augustus related to Julius Caesar?

4 Who was elected president of nationalist China in 1928?

5 What item of clothing distinguished the supporters of the Italian hero Garibaldi?

6 Judge Jeffreys presided over the trials, in 1685, following which rebellion?

7 In 1469, the marriage of Ferdinand and Isabella led to the unification of which two ancient Spanish kingdoms?

8 A wreath or chaplet of which plant was awarded to the victors in the ancient Olympic Games?

9 In which South American country's liberation did José de San Martín and Bernardo O'Higgins play major roles?

10 Whose harsh treatment of the Scots at Culloden earned him the epithet 'Butcher'?

11 Who was the first woman in Britain to qualify in and practise medicine?

12 What name was first given to partisans working as spies and saboteurs in Madrid in the Spanish Civil War?

1 Which plant is reputed to scream when plucked?

2 In the song, who adored Jake the plumber?

3 What is the name of a piece of territory entirely enclosed within foreign territory?

4 In which sport does each team have two guards, two tackles and two ends?

5 The great red spot is a feature of which planet?

6 In which country are the headquarters of the North Atlantic Treaty Organisation?

7 In which position are the sails of a dinghy when it is being sailed 'goose-winged'?

8 Which biblical character referred to his three friends as 'miserable comforters'?

9 What is the chemical symbol for ozone?

10 What was the design on the reverse of the fifty pence piece issued to celebrate Britain's entry into the Common Market?

11 According to Shakespeare, in which battle were 10,000 Frenchmen killed and only twenty-nine Englishmen?

12 Which parliamentary seat did Roy Jenkins win for the SDP in 1982?

# GAME 4

## GENERAL KNOWLEDGE (1)

1 Which country's flag is green with no markings or symbols whatever?

2 Of which international organisation was Avery Brundage the president from 1952 to 1972?

3 Which island is linked to Brooklyn by the Verrazano Narrows Bridge in New York?

4 In binary notation, how many bits are there to a byte?

5 Which word connects a bird, a wizard and an aircraft engine?

6 Inner Temple, Middle Temple and Lincoln's Inn are three of the Inns of Court. Name the fourth.

7 According to Christian legend, what was displayed on the veil of Saint Veronica?

8 What is the modern name for the ancient city of Edo?

9 How many pairs of chromosomes does a human being possess?

10 What is the original Greek meaning of the word 'martyr'?

11 Which British artist and engraver produced a series of pictures entitled *A Harlot's Progress*?

12 Which planet in the solar system has a 'day' which is longer than its 'year'?

## POP MUSIC

1   What was Adam and the Ants' first top ten hit?

2   Which composer's name was used for a song which reached number one in the spring of 1986?

3   Who sang about 'a dedicated follower of fashion'?

4   Which grocer was the subject of the 1967 number two hit *Excerpt From a Teenage Opera*?

5   About whom was Johnny Wakelin singing in his 1975 hit *Black Superman*?

6   Norman Greenbaum was a 'one-hit wonder'. What was his record, which got to number one in 1970?

7   In 1981, who leapt from number twenty-two to number one with *Green Door*?

8   Name one of the two singles in which David Bowie mentions Major Tom.

9   From which album did Queen's *Bohemian Rhapsody* come?

10  Who had a number one British hit single with *House of Fun*?

11  What name did Tom Bailey, Alannah Currie and Joe Leeway take when they joined forces?

12  How did the Motown record label get its name?

1 At the very end of *Planet of the Apes* what does Charlton Heston see half-buried in the sand?

2 What was the name of the Beatles' first film, in 1964?

3 Which film is subtitled 'Or How I Learned to Stop Worrying and Love the Bomb'?

4 Who first portrayed Dracula in a talkie?

5 Bill Forsyth's film *Comfort and Joy* is set in Glasgow and concerns rivalry within which business?

6 Al Jolson, Danny Thomas and Neil Diamond starred in the three versions of which film?

7 *Song Without End* was a film biography of which composer?

8 From which cartoon film does the song *When you Wish Upon a Star* come?

9 In 1934, which picture won Academy Awards for best picture, best actor, best actress, best director, and best written adaptation?

10 What was the name of the play in the Mel Brooks film *The Producers*?

11 In the Fellini film *Ginger and Fred*, who plays Fred?

12 Which film company has, as its trade mark, searchlights scanning skyscraper buildings?

## LITERATURE

1 In *A Midsummer Night's Dream* what made Quince exclaim: 'Bless thee, Bottom, bless thee. Thou art translated'?

2 Whose burial is described in Charles Wolfe's poem which begins: 'Not a drum was heard, not a funeral note'?

3 What was the title of the novel by Stephen Crane about the American Civil War, which was filmed by John Huston?

4 In a French play, who writes love-letters to Roxane on behalf of someone else, although he loves her himself?

5 To whom did Queen Anne give her diamonds in *The Three Musketeers*?

6 Which two classic children's books were illustrated by Sir John Tenniel?

7 Which bird is referred to in the line: 'Thou wast not born for death, immortal bird'?

8 Under what disguise does Mr Rochester startle and fool his houseguests in *Jane Eyre*?

9 What was *The Scarlet Letter*, in the novel by Hawthorne?

10 Whose secret life was described in a short story by James Thurber?

11 In *Vanity Fair*, who married Rawdon Crawley?

12 Who is the fictional character who travels through many trials and tribulations to the Celestial City?

# THE 1970s

1 In 1976, who became Britain's first world men's figure skating champion?

2 Which celebrated world championship contest took place between July and September 1972, in Reykjavik?

3 In 1976, John Avildsen won an Oscar as best director for which film?

4 The country house of Lord Rosebery was sold in 1977. What was it called?

5 Which member of the Royal Family was assassinated in August 1979?

6 Which Swedish group won the Eurovision Song Contest in 1974?

7 Which American vice-president resigned in 1973, in the face of criminal charges?

8 What was the name of the giraffe who collapsed and later died at Marwell Zoo, near Winchester, in 1977?

9 Which athlete broke the 800m and 1500m world records in Oslo in July 1979?

10 Who, in 1975, recorded *Still Crazy After All These Years*?

11 At which American university were four students shot dead in May 1970?

12 What was the subject of the referendum held in Britain in 1975?

1　Which East European state has an offical language closely related to Finnish?

2　The island group, formerly called the New Hebrides, is now known as which country?

3　Which two rivers form most of the border between East Germany and Poland?

4　Which bridge connects the Doge's palace in Venice with the state prisons and place of execution?

5　Which two countries are divided by the 38th parallel?

6　Which West Indian island is occupied by the Dominican Republic and Haiti?

7　Which pinkish monolith, 1100ft high, 6 miles around, in Northern Territory, Australia, has magical significance for the Aborigines?

8　Of which group of islands in the Indian Ocean is Mahé the main island?

9　The Russian city of Nizhni Novgorod has been renamed to celebrate which of its famous sons?

10　In which country is parliament called the Folketing?

11　On Ordnance Survey maps, what do small black arrows overprinted on roads indicate?

12　In which modern country are the biblical Tyre and Sidon?

## SPORT

1  Since the First World War, only one athlete has successfully defended the Olympic 1500m title, winning the gold medal at consecutive games. Who was he?

2  Which American was the first long jumper to jump more than 8m?

3  Which international sport is administered by FINA?

4  At which Olympic sport does competition take place over 90, 70, 60, 50 and 30m?

5  Only two players in a netball team are allowed to score. Who are they?

6  Who was Charlotte Verney's co-driver during the Paris–Dakar Rally, in January 1982?

7  In competitive sailing, which letter on the sail indicates that the boat is British?

8  Which English-trained horse won the Arlington Million horse race, in August 1985?

9  In which sport do you have penthouses, hazard sides and galleries?

10  Which international rugby union side is nicknamed 'the Pumas'?

11  Which British racing driver won the World Grand Prix championship in 1958?

12  Where were the 1980 winter Olympics held?

1 Who is the patron saint of policemen, paratroopers and grocers?

2 Which animal yields the fur called nutria?

3 'Bailiwick' describes an area administered by a bailiff. Where, in the United Kingdom, is the term still used?

4 Which organisation, founded in 1865, has the motto 'Blood and Fire'?

5 What humane operation began on 1 July 1948 and lasted for 462 days?

6 Which Holy Roman Emperor was nicknamed 'Barbarossa'?

7 Which Greek playwright died after being hit on the head by a tortoise dropped by an eagle?

8 Where could you find Robin Hood, Malkin and Moriscos in the same group?

9 How many people are required to play nine men's morris?

10 In which year was TIM, the speaking clock, introduced by the GPO?

11 Architecturally, how are the cathedrals of Chester and Chichester different from other British cathedrals?

12 In India, what is a 'dhobi'?

# GAME 5

## GENERAL KNOWLEDGE (1)

1 Which turn of the century Chicago bartender gave his name to any drink which has a knock-out effect on the imbiber?

2 For their involvement in which plot were John Wright, Christopher Wright and Thomas Winter executed?

3 Who wrote *Alexander's Ragtime Band*?

4 What is the essential difference between the target areas for foil and épée fencing?

5 Which of the seven wonders of the ancient world was built by a ruler's widow?

6 Which television fictional character has space enemies called Mysterons?

7 Who was known as 'the last of the red-hot mamas'?

8 On stairways, the horizontal part of the stair is called the 'tread'. What is the vertical board called?

9 What is the name of the bird in the cartoon strip *Peanuts*?

10 What name is given to the right to enjoy unobstructed light from windows which have had a continued existence of at least twenty years?

11 What happens to the purchase price at a Dutch auction?

12 The Life Guards and the Blues and Royals combine to make which military formation?

## TELEVISION

1 Who is the owner of the holiday camp in *Hi-De-Hi!*?

2 Where do Karl Malden and Michael Douglas police the city?

3 In an episode of *Fawlty Towers*, Manuel had a pet called Basil. What was Basil?

4 Who asks the questions on *Winner Takes All*?

5 Who used to fire the shot in *The Golden Shot*?

6 Who is the leader of the *Fairly Secret Army*?

7 In which popular American series of the 1950s did Broderick Crawford popularise the phrase 'ten four'?

8 What is the family surname in the series *No Place Like Home*?

9 What is the longest-running musical programme on British television?

10 What was the surname of the Western hero *Cheyenne*?

11 In the BBC series *Sorry!*, what is Ronnie Corbett's profession?

12 In the series *M\*A\*S\*H*, what do the initials M.A.S.H. stand for?

## CLASSICAL MUSIC

1   In Beethoven's *Fidelio*, what is Fidelio's real name?

2   Whose second symphony, composed in 1914, includes the sound of Big Ben?

3   What was the first opera by an American-born composer to be performed at La Scala?

4   What music was inspired by paintings by the artist Victor Hartmann?

5   What pseudonym was used by the English composer Philip Heseltine?

6   Which nineteenth-century violinist was so technically skilful that he was said to have made a bargain with Satan?

7   Which of Verdi's operas contains the popular Chorus of the Hebrew slaves – 'Va Pensiero'?

8   For which blind English composer did Eric Fenby write down the music?

9   Of which opera is Captain Macheath the hero?

10  In Tchaikovsky's *Swan Lake*, what is the name of the princess who is turned into a swan by the magician Rothbart?

11  Which opera by Saint-Saëns is set in Palestine?

12  The term *scherzo* is frequently heard in a musical context. What is the literal meaning of *scherzo* in Italian?

1 What is the name of the instrument fitted in lorries, which is nicknamed 'the spy in the cab'?

2 What was the name of the British airship which crashed in northern France in 1930, killing forty-seven people?

3 Which British car, introduced in 1948, was the first to sell a million?

4 Which city was the first to be linked with Paris by the TGV high-speed train?

5 What was the first large ocean-going ship to be built of iron?

6 How did Charles Rolls of Rolls and Royce die in 1910?

7 Two airlines merged to form British Airways. One was BEA – what was the other?

8 The company originally called Swallow Sidecars developed into which car-manufacturing company?

9 In 1911, for what form of transport was Bumper Harris, a man with a wooden leg, employed to demonstrate and instil confidence in the faint-hearted public?

10 What was the correct designation of the car known as the Tin Lizzie?

11 The coaches of which railway company were coloured brown and cream?

12 In 1931, a Supermarine S6 seaplane won a prestigious trophy outright for Britain. What was the name of the trophy?

## POP MUSIC

1 Which member of Bronski Beat split from the group in summer 1985?

2 What was the Erroll Garner tune with which Johnny Mathis and Ray Stevens both had hits?

3 In 1967, who had their first chart entry with *New York Mining Disaster 1941*?

4 Which song, by Slade, was released in six separate years, between 1973 and 1984?

5 Who, in a song, invented medicinal compound?

6 Who left The Commodores to establish a successful solo career?

7 Who jumped off Tallahassee Bridge?

8 Before pursuing a successful solo career, Alison Moyet was part of a duo. What was it called?

9 Which group had a hit with *Substitute* in 1966 and 1976?

10 According to the song: 'You load sixteen tons and what do you get'?

11 In 1969, what was Creedence Clearwater Revival's only number one hit in Britain?

12 In 1979, which group didn't like Mondays?

## FOOD AND DRINK

1 Who said: 'Claret is the liquor for boys; port for men; but he who aspires to be a hero must drink brandy'?

2 To westerners, what is unusual about the Japanese dish *sashimi*?

3 Which cake is named after a legendary lady from Bath?

4 Which important germ-destroying process takes place at a temperature of approximately 63°C?

5 In which country did chop suey originate as an imitation Chinese dish?

6 What is the name of the popular blue-veined cheese named after a village near Milan?

7 Which salad of celery, apples and nuts shares its name with a New York hotel?

8 In culinary terminology, what is dredging?

9 A favourite tipple among Tartar tribesmen was *koumiss*. What was *koumiss* made from?

10 From which part of the world did tomatoes originally come?

11 What is a tisane?

12 If you cook pasta '*al dente*' what does it mean?

## LIVING WORLD

1  What has three hearts, eight arms and a skirt?

2  Bempton Cliffs, in Yorkshire, form the only British mainland colony of which bird?

3  What is the name given to a colony or breeding ground of seals?

4  What is the name of the air-filled sac by which a fish maintains its buoyancy?

5  Of which garden flower is heartsease a wild variety?

6  What is the largest member of the shark family?

7  Which animal's name literally means river horse?

8  Which breed of dog takes its name from the Russian word meaning fast or swift?

9  Birds have no teeth. Specifically, which internal organ grinds up their food?

10 What type of amphibians are the crested and palmate, both of which are native to Britain?

11 What colour is the wild canary?

12 What is the name of the larval stage of the crane-fly?

1 How many embossed marks make up each letter in the Braille system?

2 Which watery novel and film is set in the seaside resort of Amity?

3 What name is given to the Chinese salutation whereby the forehead is touched to the ground?

4 Which Greek mathematician proposed: 'that two parallel lines, infinitely extended, will not meet'?

5 To what notes are the four strings of a violin normally tuned?

6 Which was the tenth country to join the EEC?

7 Who was the present Queen's first prime minister?

8 The name of this port means 'the haven of peace' and it was the former capital of German East Africa. How is it known today?

9 Who was burned at the stake in 1431, and canonised in 1920?

10 Sabin vaccine is taken orally as immunisation against which disease?

11 Which acid is also called vitriol?

12 Which city has a football club nicknamed the 'Red Imps' after the carved stone imp in its cathedral?

# GAME 6

1 Which famous murderer was apprehended by Chief Inspector Dew and Detective Sergeant Mitchell on 31 July 1910?

2 Which religious sect publishes *The Watch Tower*?

3 In Shakespeare, who was described as: 'A fellow of infinite jest, of most excellent fancy'?

4 Which is Britain's most northerly motorway?

5 If you mixed saltpetre, charcoal and sulphur, what would you get?

6 Who sang about an *A-Bomb In Wardour Street*?

7 How much notice would you have to give of intention to marry at Gretna Green?

8 What name did Nyasaland assume on independence?

9 Which metal is obtained from the ore called cinnabar?

10 Which English seaside resort was popularised by Dr Richard Russell's *A Dissertation on the Use of Sea-water*?

11 What is the name of the tune to which the hymn *All People that on Earth do Dwell* is commonly sung?

12 In the expression 'kith and kin', what does kith mean?

1   In *The Godfather* which one of Don Corleone's sons was shot to death at a toll-gate?

2   What was Disney's first feature-length all-cartoon film?

3   Which 1963 British film, starring Tom Courtenay, features the firm of undertakers, Shadrack and Duxbury?

4   Before *A Passage to India*, David Lean had not made a film for fourteen years. What was the title of his previous film?

5   Who played the part of Julian Kaye in *American Gigolo*?

6   Which group of nine child actors, led by Huntz Hall, appeared in forty-eight low-budget pictures in the post-war years?

7   In which film did Laurence Olivier declare: 'I am the Mahdi, the Expected One'?

8   The film *Chariots of Fire* concerned the Olympic Games of which year?

9   John Wayne won an Oscar for his role as a one-eyed marshal. What was the name of the character?

10  In *Whatever Happened to Baby Jane?*, who is served a rat for lunch by Bette Davis?

11  In which Alfred Hitchcock film did James Stewart play a detective with a fear of heights?

12  Which 1973 François Truffaut film won an Oscar for best foreign film?

1   Only two players scored goals for England in the 1986 World Cup finals. Who were they?

2   What is the maximum number of players in an ice-hockey team allowed on the ice at any one time?

3   A polo team is split into two groups. What are they called?

4   Who was the first English footballer to play over 100 times for his country?

5   Which international sport has a playing area of 9ft by 5ft?

6   Which American smashed the women's world mile record in Zürich in August 1985?

7   Which was the only club to win the FA Cup twice during the seventies?

8   For which country did Maharajah Ranjitsinhji play test cricket?

9   Which Soviet gymnast won three gold medals in the 1972 Olympics?

10  Who was knocked out by Frank Bruno in the first round of their WBA heavyweight final eliminator in 1986?

11  While ice-hockey is the most popular sport in Canada, which game is its official national sport?

12  In major darts competitions, what is the score at the start of the match?

1   What name was given to the anti-Catholic riots of 1780?

2   In 1865, Nathan Forrest became the first leader of which American secret society?

3   What was the name of the Turkish Empire which lasted from the fourteenth to the twentieth century?

4   Which pretender to the English throne, claiming to be Richard, Duke of York, was executed by Henry VII in 1499?

5   Which household utility did Sir John Harrington first describe in a 1596 publication?

6   In the 1880s, what did Annie Chapman, Elizabeth Stride and Mary Kelly have in common?

7   Whose Italian secretary was murdered at Holyrood House by Darnley?

8   During the Second World War who was the Japanese counterpart of Lord Haw-Haw?

9   Which British European possession did Germany take over in 1890?

10   In which hunting lodge did Marie Vetsera and Rudolph of Austria commit suicide in 1889?

11   What nickname was given to the specially raised force of auxilliary military police used in Ireland from 1920 to 1921?

12   Who was the American explorer who first reached the North Pole in 1909?

## FOOD AND DRINK

1   What leaves are traditionally used in making *dolmades*?

2   Which French vegetable dish consists of aubergines, cucumbers, peppers, tomatoes and onions stewed slowly in oil?

3   With which type of whisky is a Mint Julep made?

4   What is the Italian sausage which is often flavoured with garlic and whose name is derived from the Latin for salted?

5   Tabasco is a kind of sauce, but where is Tabasco?

6   What is made with bicarbonate of soda, cream of tartar and starch?

7   What is the name of the dish which consists of potatoes mashed in butter and egg and baked?

8   Nectar was the drink of the Greek gods. What was the food?

9   What forms the basis of a guacamole dip?

10  What are the two alcoholic ingredients of a sidecar cocktail?

11  Which cereal is used in scotch broth?

12  In a classical cheese soufflé, two grated cheeses are used. Name one of them.

## TELEVISION

1  Who wrote the book upon which the series *Shogun* was based?

2  Who was the voice of Charlie in *Charlie's Angels*?

3  Which drama-documentary, directed by Ken Loach, led directly to the setting up of the organisation Shelter?

4  In the 1950s series, what was the name of the Lone Ranger's horse?

5  Which British series was adapted for American television as *All in the Family*?

6  In which comedy series did Barry Evans teach English to a group of foreign students?

7  Who opened the pages of their Elektronik Komik?

8  In which series did Ian McShane play a shady antiques dealer?

9  What was the relationship between Eric Sykes and Hattie Jacques in their television series?

10  In which programme were children asked to play 'Double or Drop'?

11  What is the name of René's wife in *'Allo 'Allo!*?

12  In 1936 who became the first British television announcer?

## LITERATURE

1 Who wrote 'Come, friendly bombs, and fall on Slough'?

2 At the end of *Hamlet*, what is the name of the Norwegian prince who comes to claim the Danish throne?

3 In the poem by Browning, between which two places did the good news travel?

4 In J. M. Barrie's play, who was the resourceful butler to the Earl of Loam?

5 Whose portrait was painted by the fictional artist Basil Hallward?

6 Which character, created by Max Beerbohm, could never love anyone who loved her?

7 In Tolstoy's novel, whose lover is Count Vronsky?

8 Which play by Peter Shaffer deals with the life and death of Mozart?

9 In *A Tale of Two Cities*, who kept a knitted record of the names of her aristocratic victims?

10 Which author, born of Polish parents in the Ukraine, made his name writing novels in English, mainly of a seafaring nature?

11 Which English poet was drowned in a boating accident off the coast of Italy in 1822?

12 In *Wuthering Heights*, who marries Edgar Linton?

1   What line follows: 'Though cowards flinch and traitors sneer'?

2   In the field of nuclear energy, what does the abbreviation AGR stand for?

3   Which John Wyndham novel was filmed under the title *Village of the Damned*?

4   On 12 August 1940, who was the victim of the assassin Ramon Mercader, in Mexico?

5   In Greek mythology, who built the labyrinth which housed the Minotaur?

6   The 1986 Eurovision song contest was won by Sandra Kim representing which country?

7   What was the name of the original dog featured on the HMV record label?

8   Which radio character was played, successively, by Harry Oakes, Monty Crick, Edgar Harrison and Frank Middlemass?

9   The founder of the Church of Scientology died in January 1986. What was his name?

10  Which political philosopher's clothed skeleton is to be seen in University College, London?

11  What was the first single released by the Beatles on the Apple label?

12  At royal weddings, what name is used for the person who, in other circumstances, would be called the best man?

# GAME 7

## GENERAL KNOWLEDGE (1)

1 Which post carries a salary of £70 per annum and a butt of wine?

2 Which safety measure became compulsory in Britain on 31 January 1983?

3 In Celtic legend, who was the sister of King Arthur?

4 How many playing pieces are there in a set of dominoes?

5 What does the navy do sitting down that everyone else stands for?

6 Which mountain was first successfully climbed, in 1865, by Edward Whymper and six others?

7 Who created the fictional character called Biggles?

8 Who was the widow of Mao Tse Tung and the leader of the so-called 'Gang of Four'?

9 In the USA, what is the largest denomination dollar bill in circulation?

10 Which gas has the lowest boiling point?

11 Which body of men are the Queen's bodyguard for Scotland?

12 By what name is the International Fraternal Benefit Society of Roman Catholic Men usually known?

1   Which event of international significance was proclaimed by Pope Urban II at the Council of Clermont on 27 November 1095?

2   Who was the first Labour prime minister to form a government?

3   Who died in the Saint Bartholomew's Day Massacre of 1572?

4   Although he ruled England, this man's body lies in an unknown grave and his head is in a college in Cambridge. Who was he?

5   In the 1920s, whose slogan was: 'Not a penny off the pay, not a minute on the day'?

6   Whose trial, on a charge of libelling Oscar Wilde, was to lead to Wilde himself going to prison?

7   What diplomatic post was held by Sir William Hamilton, husband of Lady Emma Hamilton, who became the mistress of Horatio Nelson?

8   Roman gladiators took their name from the gladius. What type of weapon was a gladius?

9   Which eighteenth-century astronomer pioneered the centigrade scale of temperature?

10  Which successful London entrepreneur, politician and philanthropist married Alice Fitzwarren?

11  Who was shot during a performance of *Our American Cousin* on 14 April 1865?

12  When the Spanish, led by Cortez, invaded Mexico, who was the Aztec emperor?

## POP MUSIC

1. In 1982 who asked: 'Ullo John, gotta new motor'?

2. Who played with both Cream and The Yardbirds?

3. What was the Glitter Band's first hit single after the departure of Gary Glitter?

4. What was the title of Village People's only number one single in Britain?

5. Who teamed up with Cliff Richard to have a number one hit with *Living Doll* in 1986?

6. On the sleeve of Michael Jackson's *Off the Wall* album, which two items of his clothing stand out from the rest?

7. Who had a hit in 1979 with *Day Trip to Bangor*?

8. Who not only played all the instruments, but also arranged and produced Cliff Richard's single *She's So Beautiful*?

9. What was the first of Paul Simon's *50 Ways to Leave Your Lover*?

10. In which year was the Woodstock Music and Arts Fair held?

11. Which singer's middle name was Nesta?

12. With which disc did the Animals score a number one in the United States?

## LIVING WORLD

1   If a horse is 16 hands high, how tall is it in inches?

2   What is the name of the green pigment used by plants to carry out the process of photosynthesis?

3   Which is the smallest reptile native to Britain?

4   Which creatures are listed in the *Red Data Book*?

5   How many segments does a caterpillar have?

6   What forms the principal diet of the starfish known as crown of thorns?

7   What is the name given to eyes composed of many facets, which flies and butterflies, etc, have?

8   Which native animal of South America, introduced in 1929 for fur farming, is now considered a pest in East Anglia?

9   What animal is thought to be the closest living relative of the extinct quagga?

10   What fish is characterised by red or orange spots on its upper surface?

11   What is the correct name for a kangaroo's pouch?

12   Which animal has earned the nickname of 'the glutton'?

## CINEMA

1 Which film was advertised with the slogan 'You will believe a man can fly'?

2 Who starred as *The Pilgrim* and *The Adventurer*?

3 Who were Tom and Jerry's original animators?

4 In which 1938 film does Miss Froy write her name on a steamed-up train window?

5 In which city was *The Third Man* set?

6 What was the title of Otto Preminger's epic film of the birth of the State of Israel?

7 In which film did Yul Brynner play a robot western gunfighter?

8 On which Shakespeare play was Kurosawa's *Throne of Blood* based?

9 Which actress starred opposite Humphrey Bogart in *The Maltese Falcon*?

10 Which film starring Marlene Dietrich opens with gun shots and a sign reading 'Welcome to Bottleneck'?

11 In which film did Peter Sellers play a communist shop steward?

12 Who directed the Keystone Kops comedies?

1 What was banned from British television screens on 1 August 1965?

2 Name the London car dealer who disappeared in January 1965, in strange circumstances.

3 During the 1960s a group of Salvation Army musicians had two hit records. Under what name did they record?

4 Which South Atlantic island had all its inhabitants evacuated to Britain in 1961, following the eruption of a volcano?

5 Which man controlled the ill-fated Fire, Auto and Marine Insurance Company?

6 The First Secretary of the Czechoslovakian Communist Party was deposed in 1969 because of his policy of liberalisation. Who was he?

7 In 1966, Captain Ridgeway and Sergeant 'Chay' Blyth became the first Britons to perform which feat?

8 Which African politican became Premier of Bechuanaland in 1965, and President of Botswana in 1966?

9 What name was given to the massive offensive launched by the Vietcong against South Vietnam in 1968?

10 In 1962, which prince married Sofia, daughter of King Paul of Greece?

11 Which controversial construction was begun on 19 November 1961?

12 Which famous American penitentiary was closed on 21 March 1963?

## GEOGRAPHY

1 Which is the highest point on Bodmin Moor, Cornwall?

2 Where are the Eastern and the Western Ghats?

3 Tobruk was the scene of heavy fighting in the Second World War. In which country is Tobruk?

4 Which of the counties of Northern Ireland does not border Lough Neagh?

5 The boundary between Suffolk and Cambridgeshire cuts through which racecourse?

6 In which country are the Drakensberg mountains?

7 Why is a maelstrom dangerous?

8 Which two countries are linked by the Khyber Pass?

9 Of the main Channel Islands, which is the most westerly?

10 The official language of Haiti is that of the colonial power to which it once belonged. Which language is it?

11 In which country is Lidice, the village destroyed by the Nazis in 1942?

12 Of which country is the Bio-Bio the longest river?

1 On what river does London in Ontario, Canada, stand?

2 Which Middle Eastern leader was assassinated on 6 October 1981?

3 Which day commemorates the Washing of the Feet and the Last Supper?

4 The Owl and the Pussycat went to sea, but who married them?

5 Which actor compiled an Almanac of Astounding Information entitled *Not Many People Know That*?

6 What do psychologists mean by the abbreviation REM which occurs during sleep?

7 What had Mole been doing all morning at the start of *The Wind in the Willows*?

8 Why is January so called?

9 Since 1970, what do the initials CPRE stand for?

10 Which lady flier, in 1930, hit the headlines through her epic flight from England to Australia in a De Havilland Gipsy Moth aeroplane?

11 Which Scottish music-hall singer is best remembered for *Roamin' in the Gloamin'*?

12 In Norse mythology, how many legs did Odin's horse, Sleipnir, have?

# GAME 8

## GENERAL KNOWLEDGE (1)

1  What was the name of the Italian cruise ship which was hijacked by Palestinians in 1985?

2  Who first spoke the words known as 'The Magnificat'?

3  Which political leader is buried in the churchyard at Colombey-les-deux-Eglises?

4  In the *Old Testament*, Esau sold his birthright for a mess of pottage. Who bought it?

5  Which big band leader's first names were Edward Kennedy?

6  How many demi-semiquavers are there in a minim?

7  What name is given to the Pope's personal military guards?

8  In which village did Jesus turn water into wine at a wedding?

9  What was written on the price tag of the Mad Hatter's hat?

10  Which French author's work was turned into an opera when Verdi wrote *Rigoletto*?

11  Who lost her heart to a starship trooper in 1978?

12  If you hit a blot before it makes a point, which game are you playing?

## SPORT

1 What did Pickles do in 1966?

2 What is a flying mare?

3 Which two things stand 28in high and 66ft apart?

4 Mick the Miller and Patricia's Hope are the only ones to have won it twice. What is it?

5 What did Santa Claus win in 1964?

6 Who won a record seven gold medals at the 1972 Olympic Games in Munich?

7 What name is given to the playing objects that are used in curling?

8 Which future world heavyweight champion won the Olympic light heavyweight title in 1960?

9 Who won the Pot Black championship in 1984?

10 Which young female British swimmer won two gold medals in the 1986 Commonwealth Games?

11 Which horse-racing institution was founded in 1916 by Lord Wavertree?

12 Who is the only Frenchman to win the world motor racing championship?

# LITERATURE

1 In which eighteenth-century book do we first meet the Yahoos?

2 Which play by Ben Jonson has the alternative title 'The Foxe'?

3 In which play by Shakespeare does a king ride a horse called Surrey until it is killed?

4 Which novel by Wilkie Collins tells the story of a diamond originally stolen from an Indian shrine and of its eventual recovery?

5 Which of Chaucer's female pilgrims wore a brooch with the words *Amor Vincit Omnia* beneath a letter 'A'?

6 The British aircraft engineer N. S. Norway, who died in 1960, is better known as which novelist?

7 Which Hemingway novel is set during the Spanish Civil War?

8 Who wrote the Horatio Hornblower novels?

9 In Shaw's *Pygmalion* who is wooed by Freddy Eynsford Hill?

10 What was the name of the perfect state written about by Sir Thomas More?

11 In *The Adventures of Tom Sawyer*, who murders the town doctor and is later found dead in a cave?

12 What is an 'eponymous' hero?

1  In *The Irish RM* What is the name of Major Yeates's housekeeper?

2  In which series did Ian Dury play the manager of an East London pool hall?

3  How are Fonzie and Chachi related in *Happy Days*?

4  What is the name of the comedy series in which Richard Briers plays a vicar taking on a more challenging parish?

5  When Barry got married in *Auf Wiedersehen Pet*, what was unusual about the best man?

6  Which character did Jean Marsh play in *Upstairs, Downstairs*?

7  Who was the first presenter of *Monitor*, who went on to become Director General of the BBC?

8  In *Coronation Street*, how did Ken Barlow's first wife die?

9  Russell Hunter played the lonely friend of which professional killer?

10  Heinz Wolff presents an annual contest of ingenuity on BBC 2. What is it called?

11  Buddy Ebsen, eccentric dancer, portrayed Jed Clampett in which popular series?

12  In which series does Bill Bixby turn into Lou Ferrigno when angered?

## FOOD AND DRINK

1  Which Italian sauce is made with basil, garlic, oil and pine kernels?

2  From which country does chutney originate?

3  In what state is any drink which is served frappé?

4  How would you cook Chicken Maryland?

5  What is pumpernickel?

6  Which Spanish wine-producing region is divided into Alta, Alavesa and Baja?

7  Mysore, Blue Mountain and Teaberry are varieties of what?

8  Of which tree is the filbert the fruit?

9  What is the usual chief constituent of brawn?

10  What French name is given to an earthenware pot or jar used for pâté or savoury mixture?

11  In English cooking, which word, derived from old French for 'boiling thoroughly' now means 'boiling preliminary to further cooking'?

12  What type of food are sloke, dulse and carrageen?

# THE 1960s

1  Who won the British Grand Prix a record five times between 1962 and 1967?

2  In which country was President Ben Bella overthrown in a military coup?

3  In which year was Prince Edward born?

4  Which new method of detection was first used by British police in the capture of Edwin Bush in 1961?

5  The entertainer Nikolai Poliakoff was awarded the OBE in 1963. How was he better known?

6  Which shops were legalised on 1 May 1961?

7  What was the name of the farm in Buckinghamshire used as a hideout by the Great Train Robbers in 1963?

8  What was the name of the black militant leader who was shot dead in Harlem in 1965?

9  In 1965, Hawker Siddeley Dynamics developed a space launcher missile in conjunction with the European Launcher Development Organisation. What was its name?

10  In 1961, who was enthroned as the 100th Archbishop of Canterbury?

11  What name was given to the 1969 white paper on industrial relations, never, in fact, implemented?

12  Who was the Australian prime minister who drowned in a swimming accident in December 1967?

## CLASSICAL MUSIC

1 Which ballet, with music by Delibes, is subtitled 'The Girl with Enamel Eyes'?

2 Which of Schubert's symphonies was *The Unfinished*?

3 Who wrote the words, Gilbert or Sullivan?

4 Which choral work by Handel includes a *Pastoral Symphony*?

5 In the symphony orchestra there are four instruments in the string family: violin, cello, viola and what is the fourth?

6 Which nickname links a Beethoven piano concerto, a Haydn string quartet and a Strauss waltz?

7 Which well-known tune from Bach's *Suite No 3 in D* is played on the lowest string of the violin?

8 Which fairy story has been the basis of operas by Rossini, Massenet and Wolf-Ferrari, and a ballet by Prokofiev?

9 Which orchestral overture and suite by Sibelius has the same name as a province in southern Finland?

10 Of which orchestra was Leopold Stokowski the principal conductor for almost thirty years?

11 Which oratorio by Elgar takes a poem by Cardinal Newman as its text?

12 In Offenbach's opera, who had three loves called Olympia, Giulietta and Antonia?

1 At the start of a game of bridge, which is the lowest undoubled game call?

2 What did Lloyd George describe as 'Mr Balfour's poodle'?

3 What make of car got its name from the fact that it was made in Spain (and France) and designed by a Swiss engineer?

4 What is unusual about the musical piece *Four minutes thirty-three seconds*, written by John Cage in 1952?

5 What name was given to the chief official of a district in Nazi Germany?

6 What type of weapon is carried by Yeoman Warders (or Beefeaters)?

7 In which country is the fado a type of folk song?

8 In law, what is the word used to describe the offence of trying to bribe or influence a jury corruptly?

9 In 1970, Thor Heyerdahl crossed the Atlantic in a craft named Ra-2. What was it made of?

10 Who was the famous pupil of Anne Sullivan?

11 In photography, some cameras record on the film a view which is slightly different from that seen through the viewfinder. What is this difference called?

12 What is indicated by a blue circular roadsign with 30 in white numerals?

# GAME 9

1  What is the official religion of the United States?

2  Apart from Paul McCartney and Wings, who had a hit with *Let 'Em In*?

3  Which Scottish firth lies between Dornoch Firth and Moray Firth?

4  What is the title of Lord Grade's brother who is also a life peer?

5  In the Royal Navy, what does the term 'number one' or 'Jimmy the one' refer to?

6  What is $H_2SO_4$?

7  Between which two planets do the asteroids of the asteroid belt mainly lie?

8  Which Australian state capital is named after a British prime minister?

9  What was the name of the snail in *The Magic Roundabout*?

10  Which American hero is known in song as the 'king of the wild frontier'?

11  Who are the indigenous people inhabiting northern Scandinavia?

12  Which drink becomes Irish if you add an 'e' to its name?

## LIVING WORLD

1  Is the bathroom loofah animal, vegetable or mineral?

2  Which is the world's largest carnivorous land mammal?

3  The sale of the reptile *Testudo graeca* as a pet is now licensed and restricted. How is this animal more commonly known?

4  Which ancestor of the farmyard chicken is still to be found in Asia?

5  What shape are the cells of a honeycomb?

6  Cattle cannot be reared over large parts of Africa because of the presence of which insect?

7  To which order of mammals do shrews and moles belong?

8  Which is the slowest-moving land mammal?

9  Which continent is the original habitat of the grey squirrel?

10  What constitutes the sole diet of the osprey?

11  What is the product of rattan palm, often used in furniture making?

12  Which animal, like a large shrew, is native to both Australia and New Guinea?

# GEOGRAPHY

1 Which city in Tuscany is the centre of the Italian marble industry?

2 Which thoroughfare on Manhattan Island is known as the centre of the New York advertising business?

3 In South America, what is a pueblo?

4 Which is the largest of the Mediterranean islands?

5 Which feature of the English landscape is partly the result of the flooding of the river Bure and its tributaries into former peat-diggings?

6 Where are the Spenser mountains and the Garvie mountains?

7 Which Asian country has an administrative capital city called Vientiane?

8 In which European country is there a province called Luxembourg?

9 Which point on the Scottish mainland lies closest to Northern Ireland?

10 Viti Levu and Vanua Levu are the largest islands in which island republic?

11 What is the name of the region of the southern oceans where the strong prevailing westerlies blow?

12 What is the main town on the Isle of Sheppey?

## CINEMA

1 Which child film star appeared as Puck in the 1935 film *A Midsummer Night's Dream*?

2 What was the sequel to *Romancing the Stone* called?

3 What is the name of the valley which John Ford used as the setting for the film *Stagecoach*?

4 In which film was Charlie Allnutt the leading male character?

5 Who wrote the lyrics for the Oscar-winning song *Moon River*?

6 Who played the husband and wife team of lawyers in the 1949 film *Adam's Rib*?

7 What is the name of the motel in *Psycho*?

8 What was Elvis Presley's first film?

9 In which film did Julie Andrews portray Gertrude Lawrence?

10 Who directed *The Railway Children*?

11 Which American film actress was known as 'the Blonde Bombshell'?

12 Which musical film starring Natalie Wood and Richard Beymer won eleven Oscars?

## HISTORY

1   Which explorer set out in 1914 to cross Antarctica, but was foiled when his ship was caught in the ice and crushed?

2   Who was the wife of Leofric, Earl of Mercia?

3   Which high-ranking Dominican, born in 1420, was notorious for his work for the Spanish Inquisition?

4   On which island did the mutineers from the *Bounty* settle in 1790?

5   Of which English city was Eric Bloodaxe the last Viking king?

6   Of which British tribe was Boudicca the queen?

7   Which Moslem military leader was the antagonist of Richard I during the Third Crusade?

8   At the end of the eighteenth century, in order to prevent which disease did the Royal Navy issue daily rations of lime or lemon juice?

9   What was the name of the moderate socialist party in Russia, which was suppressed in 1922?

10   Which British prime minister brought back 'peace with honour' from Germany in 1878?

11   What was the name of Alfred the Great's kingdom?

12   By the Treaty of Windsor, signed in 1386, England and which other country became permanent allies?

## TELEVISION

1   What is the first name of Pauline and Arthur's baby in *EastEnders*?

2   Before he became prime minister, of which government ministry was Jim Hacker the head?

3   Who are Rick, Neil, Mike and Vivien?

4   Who became famous for his 'swingometer' during general election programmes?

5   Which television duo had a horse called Hercules?

6   Which drama series was based on the fortunes of a demobbed RAF stores clerk and his family?

7   What is the name of Dorothy's mother in *Golden Girls*?

8   What was the name of the chief of the federal special squad played by Robert Stack in *The Untouchables*?

9   In which fictional town was *Doctor Finlay's Casebook* set?

10  Which ITV series begins each episode with the words, 'Gentlemen, you are about to enter the most fascinating sphere of police work – the world of forensic medicine'?

11  Which controversial drama-documentary caused a four-month diplomatic breach between Britain and Saudi Arabia in 1980?

12  Gounod's *Funeral March of a Marionette* was used as the rather sinister theme tune of which director's mystery series?

1  In a bottle of wine, what is the ullage?

2  What is the traditional Thanksgiving dessert in the United States?

3  In which country is *kvass* a traditional drink similar to beer?

4  What other name is used for endive?

5  Which wine races into the country each November?

6  What are the ingredients of marzipan?

7  In which country is the Barossa Valley, famous for its vineyards and its wine festival?

8  If you were in a Swiss restaurant, what would you most likely see cooked in a raclette?

9  If you were preparing *coquilles Saint-Jacques*, what type of seafood should you buy?

10  In what is the meat of beef Wellington finally encased before it goes into the oven?

11  Which two spirits are combined to make a B and B?

12  What variety of fish is a bloater?

1 How many ghosts of Christmas are in *A Christmas Carol*?

2 Who was the supreme allied commander-in-chief on D-Day?

3 What is Flemish bond?

4 What is made by infusing carbonic acid gas into water under pressure?

5 Where in County Meath was the seat of the kings of Ireland?

6 Which prison, near Rochester in Kent, gave its name in 1902 to a system of punishing young offenders?

7 In geometry, what name is given to a circular arc subtending an angle of 90 degrees?

8 Which Irish playwright wrote *Juno and the Paycock*?

9 The Amalienborg is the royal residence in which capital city?

10 Which famous nineteenth-century trapeze artist is commemorated in a suitable garment?

11 For what do the initials of the P & O Steam Navigation Company stand?

12 With which religion is the Juggernaut associated?

# GAME 10

## GENERAL KNOWLEDGE (1)

1 Which author's fictional characters met regularly in Mindy's Restaurant?

2 Who starred with her father in the film *Paper Moon*?

3 If somebody were born on Christmas Day, what would be their birth sign?

4 Who was the newspaper heiress kidnapped in 1974 by the Symbionese Liberation Army?

5 *Make Believe* and *Old Man River* are songs from which musical?

6 At sea, if you took the first watch, at what time would you start?

7 From which language do the words parka and anorak derive?

8 What was the name of the Rolls-Royce car produced between 1906 and 1925?

9 Who was assassinated by James Earl Ray in April 1968?

10 In 1984, which Olympic event was won by Tessa Sanderson with a distance of 69.56m?

11 What is the full title of the organisation known as SHAPE, which has its headquarters in Brussels?

12 In knitting, what are alternate rows of plain and purl stitch called?

## LITERATURE

1 Who wrote *Portrait of the Artist as a Young Man*?

2 Who wrote *Portrait of the Artist as a Young Dog*?

3 Which play by Noël Coward features a medium called Madam Arcati?

4 Who was *The Merchant of Venice*?

5 Which nineteenth-century American writer of mystery and horror stories wrote a tale of a murder committed by an orang-utan?

6 What is the title of Dante's poem that comprises the Inferno, the Purgatorio and the Paradiso?

7 In *The Forsyte Saga*, who was Irene's second husband?

8 What was the name of 'She who must be obeyed' in Rider Haggard's book *She*?

9 Which legal character refers to his wife as 'She who must be obeyed'?

10 In Hardy's *Far from the Madding Crown*, why does the marriage arranged between Sergeant Troy and Fanny Robin not take place?

11 'Cover her face; mine eyes dazzle; she died young.' Who was she?

12 Which English novel, written in the 1920s, was not published in this country in its full version until 1960?

# CINEMA

1  Which film alien was befriended by a boy called Elliott?

2  Tyne Daly co-starred with Clint Eastwood in which Dirty Harry film?

3  In which film did Spencer Tracy play an enigmatic one-armed stranger?

4  In which Hitchcock film does Paul Newman play a nuclear scientist?

5  When Nigel Bruce played Doctor Watson which actor played Sherlock Holmes?

6  In which film did John Wayne play Davy Crockett and Richard Widmark play Jim Bowie?

7  Which poet laureate's son starred in both *My Beautiful Laundrette* and *A Room with a View*?

8  Which comedy team were the stars of the 1952 film *Lost in Alaska*?

9  Which silent-film actress made her debut in the talkies with the words: 'Give me a whiskey with ginger ale on the side, and don't be stingy, baby'?

10  Which actor directed *Staying Alive*, the sequel to *Saturday Night Fever*?

11  What is the name of the character played by Gene Hackman in *Bonnie and Clyde*?

12  In which film did Jack Nicholson play the caretaker of The Overlook Hotel?

1  Which group was *Calling all the Heroes* in 1986?

2  Who wrote the song *Help Me Make It Through The Night*?

3  Who was the only barefoot Beatle on the cover of *Abbey Road*?

4  What was the number one record on which Olivia Newton-John was backed by ELO?

5  Who had many rivers to cross in 1983?

6  Which event precipitated the final break-up of Led Zeppelin?

7  Which goddess did Bananarama sing about in 1986?

8  Of the seven Elvis Presley singles with the words 'blue' or 'blues' in the title, which was the first?

9  Who made punk rock records entitled *Give 'em Enough Rope* and *London Calling*?

10  Whose line-up includes Helen O'Hara on violin?

11  Who was the female lead singer on Steeleye Span's single *All Around My Hat*?

12  Which group did Funboy Three join on the 1982 hit *It ain't what you do, it's the way that you do it*?

## THE 1960s

1   Which national daily newspaper ceased publication in 1964?

2   Which Scottish city was affected by a serious typhoid epidemic in May and June 1964?

3   Who was the London osteopath who committed suicide at the height of the Christine Keeler scandal?

4   Under what name was Nicholas Henty-Dodd well known to television viewers and radio listeners in the 1960s?

5   Who seized power from King Idris after a military coup in 1969?

6   Which new British cathedral was consecrated in 1962?

7   Who succeeded Nikita Kruschev as prime minister of the Soviet Union in 1964?

8   Which park did the Small Faces first sing about in 1967?

9   Which horse won the Grand National in 1967, at the odds of 100–1?

10  In 1967, in which country did a coup bring an end to a monarchy and put a military junta in power?

11  British Rail was given its name in 1964; how was it previously known?

12  In 1967, what was the name of the first recipient of a human heart transplant?

1   The 1975 King George VI and Queen Elizabeth Diamond Stakes has been dubbed 'England's race of the century'. Who won the race?

2   Greg LeMond became the first American to win which major cycle race in 1986?

3   Who succeeded Torvill and Dean as British ice dance champions?

4   In which sport might you use a silver Wilkinson?

5   In which country did Brazil last win soccer's World Cup?

6   Which former world heavyweight boxing champion's real name was Arnold Raymond Cream?

7   Which cricket county has, as its emblem, six martlets?

8   Which form of athletic competition was revolutionised in the late 1960s by Dick Fosberry?

9   Who was the unfortunate bowler when Gary Sobers scored six consecutive sixes in one over in 1968?

10   What name is given to the sign-language used by race-track bookies?

11   Which game takes its name from the Gloucestershire estate of the Duke of Beaufort where it was first played in the 1860s?

12   Who won the 1985 European Grand Prix, held at Brands Hatch?

## GEOGRAPHY

1 Where in Europe can you see the mirage known locally as Fata Morgana?

2 In which seaway are the Thousand Islands?

3 What is a tarn?

4 Which city in Yugoslavia is the capital of Croatia?

5 Which is the only South American country with both Pacific and Caribbean coastlines?

6 In which of the oceans is Baffin Island?

7 Which two countries have permanent settlements on Spitsbergen?

8 Which city is the federal capital of Switzerland?

9 What is the name of the peninsula which forms about 70 per cent of the total area of Denmark?

10 What is the name of the highest lake in the world, which lies between Peru and Bolivia?

11 Cairo and Memphis are on which river of the United States?

12 Which is the most famous of the basalt caverns on the island of Staffa?

1  In which year, this century, did three popes hold office?

2  Which word was coined by the Czech playwright Karel Čapek, in 1920, to describe a man-made mechanical worker?

3  Whose persecution and assassination was performed by the inmates of the asylum of Charenton, under the direction of the Marquis de Sade?

4  Which Spanish painter's only female nude is known as the Rokeby Venus?

5  What is the name of the layer of the Earth's atmosphere in which we live?

6  What rank in the Royal Artillery corresponds to that of corporal in a line regiment?

7  In *Uncle Tom's Cabin*, what is the name of Uncle Tom's cruel master who has him beaten to death?

8  What would your profession probably be if you were an LRAM?

9  Which former British world champion boxer died in May 1966, aged thirty-seven?

10  Which tree was sacred to the Druids?

11  What name is given, in Britain, to the second Sunday in November?

12  An unfledged pigeon is known specifically by what name?

# ANSWERS

**Game 1**    General Knowledge (1)
1 Anthony Burgess.    2 Excommunication in the Roman
Catholic Church.    3 *Luftwaffe*.    4 Sir Cecil Beaton.
5 Edward Heath.    6 Smoking.    7 Marquesses.    8 Floyd
Patterson.    9 The Sirens.    10 Ammonia.    11 Lover of
horses or fond of horses.    12 Epiphany.

**Game 1**    Sport
1 A left-handed googly. (A googly is an off-break bowled
with a leg-break action.)    2 Three – 1916, 1940 and
1944.    3 Joe Davis.    4 Popping crease.    5 Squash.
6 Motor racing. (The Gordon Bennett Races preceded the
French Grand Prix).    7 Jack Dempsey and Gene
Tunney.    8 Teenoso.    9 White.    10 Tenpin bowling.
11 Pentathlon.    12 The Admiral's Cup.

**Game 1**    Food and Drink
1 Vodka    2 Yoghurt.    3 Arbroath    4 Mulling.    5 The kiwi
fruit.    6 Grill it.    7 The chive.    8 Baron of beef.
9 To bring out the flavour or intensify the natural
flavour.    10 Mulligatawny (from *milagu-tannir*).
11 Prunes and bacon.    12 Carp.

**Game 1**    History
1 'Publish and be damned!'    2 Lord Kitchener.
3 Captain Hardy.    4 Mercia.    5 The British Museum.
6 Manhattan.    7 Michael Collins.    8 Thomas à
Becket.    9 The Alamo.    10 The Man in the Iron
Mask.    11 *1066 And All That*.    12 Entente Cordiale.

**Game 1**    Pop Music
1 Wham!    2 Lady Jane.    3 None.    4 *Lucy in the Sky with
Diamonds*.    5 *My Ding-a-Ling*.    6 Paul Anka.
7 Bow Wow Wow.    8 Frankie Goes to Hollywood.
9 Dolly Parton.    10 Ian Kilminster.    11 Vincent Price.
12 The Dakotas.

**Game 1    The 1960s**
1 The American moon landing.    2 *The Sound of Music*.
3 Arkle (1964, 1965, 1966).    4 Unit Four Plus Two.
5 The Duke of Edinburgh.    6 Goldie the eagle.
7 Frances Gary Powers.    8 4–2.    9 Sheila Scott.
10 *The Times*.    11 Agadir.    12 1969.

**Game 1    Television**
1 *Hawaii Five-O*.    2 Peckham.    3 *Bonanza*.    4 1982
(November).    5 Spit.    6 The cello.    7 *The Antiques
Roadshow*.    8 *Columbo*.    9 *First Among Equals*.
10 Nora Batty.    11 Dentist.    12 Basildon Bond.

**Game 1    General Knowledge (2)**
1 Japanese (Toshihiko Seko).    2 Primordial soup or
primeval soup.    3 Lon Chaney.    4 The Troggs.
5 Atlas.    6 Sand-dancing (Egyptian).    7 Quarks.
8 Thirteen.    9 The sidewinder.    10 The Antonine
Wall.    11 *East Lynne*.    12 The *Lusitania*.

**Game 2    General Knowledge (1)**
1 Mussolini.    2 Artesian.    3 They looked back.    4 Little
Lord Fauntleroy.    5 Red blood cells.    6 Kensington
Gore.    7 Kensington Gore.    8 Byzantium (not
Constantinople).    9 The Dangerous Brothers.    10 Lord
Beaverbrook (William Maxwell Aitken).    11 He crossed a
running stream (on horseback).    12 Camp David.

**Game 2    Geography**
1 Moscow.    2 The date is put back a day.    3 South
Carolina.    4 Sussex.    5 South Africa.    6 Hanoi.
7 Andalucia.    8 Lundy.    9 Mount Sinai.
10 Patagonia.    11 The Tagus.    12 East Falkland (Port
Stanley).

**Game 2    Cinema**
1 John Wayne (playing the part of Tom Doniphon in *The
Man who Shot Liberty Valance*).    2 Oddjob.    3 Rod
Steiger.    4 King Kong.    5 Headmaster    6 Busby
Berkeley.    7 *Gypsy*.    8 Rin Tin Tin.    9 Margaret
Dumont.    10 James Mason (as Professor Oliver
Lindenbrook).    11 Ealing Studios.    12 Ingmar Bergman.

**Game 2**  Living World
1 Fat.  2 Sociable weaverbirds join together and build large collective nests.  3 Cheetah.  4 Smooth snake.
5 Carp.  6 A web-footed bird.  7 Raccoon.  8 Humming bird.  9 Shoebill or bogbird.  10 Growing towards the light.  11 Bee.  12 Capercaillie.

**Game 2**  Literature
1 Winnie The Pooh.  2 *Midnight's Children*.
3 *Rosencrantz and Guildenstern Are Dead*.  4 He stole a loaf of bread.  5 Charles Darnay (Marquis St Evrémonde).  6 Queeg.  7 Robert Burns.  8 The rats in *The Pied Piper of Hamelin*.  9 Miss Prism, the Governess.  10 *Lorna Doone*.  11 Sir Lancelot.
12 Barabbas.

**Game 2**  The 1970s
1 Chi-Chi (the panda).  2 Amnesty International.
3 Andreas (Baader) or Ulrike (Meinhof).  4 Henry Kissinger.  5 Anthony Blunt.  6 The Grand National.
7 *American Pie*.  8 *Oz*.  9 Lockheed.  10 Valéry Giscard D'Estaing.  11 *Amoco Cadiz*.  12 Value added tax.

**Game 2**  Classical Music
1 *Zadok the Priest*.  2 Floria Tosca.  3 *Billy the Kid*.  4 A recurring theme associated with a certain idea, character, scene, etc.  5 Surprise Symphony (no 94 in G).  6 Polkas (by Johann Strauss the Younger).  7 Liszt (he became the Abbé Liszt).  8 Four.  9 *Clair de Lune*.  10 Robert Schumann.  11 Paganini (Caprice in A minor no 24).
12 *Don Giovanni* by Mozart ('The Catalogue Aria').

**Game 2**  General Knowledge 2
1 Lord Peter Wimsey.  2 The (American) Declaration of Independence.  3 Sir John Vanbrugh.  4 HMS *Hermes* and HMS *Invincible*.  5 The Abbey Theatre.  6 Military police.  7 Giotto.  8 It is sloped at two different angles: the lower one steeper than the higher one.  9 The Pope's ring (it has Peter the fisherman on it).  10 Leda.
11 Eight.  12 1948.

**Game 3**   General Knowledge 1
1 Golden Miller.   2 Apollo 8.   3 Mata Hari.   4 A pale
horse.   5 Everybody.   6 An eye.   7 Colditz.   8 Salt.
9 Lara.   10 Queen Anne.   11 The beetle.   12 The
Church of Jesus Christ of Latterday Saints (the Mormon
Church).

**Game 3**   The 1960s
1 Westminster Abbey.   2 *Private Eye*.   3 George
Blake.   4 The Queen's Award to Industry.   5 Andy
Warhol.   6 John Bloom.   7 *Hair*.   8 Dr Barbara
Moore   9 Ronan Point.   10 The Kirov.   11 Cassius Clay
(Muhammad Ali).   12 Chuck Berry.

**Game 3**   Television
1 *Cheers*.   2 *When the Boat Comes In*.   3 Alice
Christine.   4 *Peyton Place*.   5 Harry Corbett.
6 All-points bulletin.   7 *The Prisoner*.   8 Desmond
Lynam.   9 John Freeman.   10 *The Fenn Street
Gang*.   11 *The Flintstones* (Fred and Wilma).
12 The cat, Jess.

**Game 3**   Classical Music
1 Kathleen Ferrier.   2 Erik Satie.   3 Radetzky.
4 *Greensleeves*.   5 The Bringer of Old Age.
6 *Turandot*.   7 Vivaldi.   8 *The Rite of Spring*.
9 Mozart.   10 *The Yeomen of the Guard*.   11 *The
Raindrop Prelude*.   12 Carl Orff (*Carmina Burana*).

**Game 3**   Sport
1 Berwick Rangers.   2 Brian Whittle (in the 400m
relay).   3 Irina Rodnina.   4 Croquet.   5 The Super Bowl
(American football).   6 Walter Swinburn.   7 12ft ×
6ft.   8 Charlie Pasarell (after a total of 112 games –
22–24, 1–6, 16–14, 6–3, 11–9. The match took 5 hours 12
minutes and was only a first round).   9 Dame Naomi
James.   10 Four.   11 Kevin Curren.   12 He was the
Russian pentathlete who was caught cheating with a
bugged épée in the fencing.

**Game 3 Transport**

1 Alcock and Brown's first non-stop crossing of the Atlantic by air.    2 The *Carpathia*.    3 The Grand Canal.
4 Aeroflot.    5 A small ship with sails and/or oars.    6 The *Brighton Belle*.    7 Howard Hughes (the Hughes H2 Hercules Flying Boat – wingspan 320ft).    8 Cabriolet (a carriage).    9 William Morris (Lord Nuffield).
10 *Locomotion*.    11 Bahrain.    12 F. W. Lanchester.

**Game 3 History**

1 Sir Thomas More.    2 Woodrow Wilson.    3 Augustus was Julius Caesar's great nephew and adopted son.
4 Chiang Kai-Shek.    5 Red shirts.    6 The Monmouth Rebellion.    7 Aragon and Castile.    8 Wild olive leaves.
9 Chile.    10 The Duke of Cumberland – Butcher Cumberland.    11 Elizabeth Garrett Anderson.    12 Fifth columnists.

**Game 3 General Knowledge (2)**

1 The mandrake.    2 *Secondhand Rose*.    3 An enclave.
4 American football.    5 Jupiter.    6 Belgium.
7 At right-angles to the boat, ie each sail sticking out on either side of the boat.    8 Job.    9 $O_3$.    10 A circular design of nine linked hands around the perimeter (value and date in the centre).    11 Agincourt.    12 Glasgow Hillhead.

**Game 4 General Knowledge (1)**

1 Libya.    2 The International Olympic Committee.
3 Staten Island.    4 Eight.    5 Merlin.    6 Gray's Inn.    7 The imprint of the face of Christ. (She wiped his face with it when he was on the way to the crucifixion.)    8 Tokyo.
9 Twenty-three pairs.    10 Witness.    11 William Hogarth.    12 Venus (it orbits the sun more quickly than it rotates once).

**Game 4**   Pop Music
1 *Dog Eat Dog*.   2 Amadeus (Mozart).   3 The Kinks.
4 Grocer Jack.   5 Muhammad Ali.   6 *Spirit in the Sky*.
7 Shakin' Stevens.   8 *Space Oddity* and *Ashes to Ashes*.
9 *Night at the Opera*.   10 Madness.   11 The Thompson
Twins.   12 From Detroit (popularly known as Motor
Town – where the record company was based until 1967).

**Game 4**   Cinema
1 The Statue of Liberty.   2 *A Hard Day's Night*.
3 *Dr Strangelove*.   4 Bela Lugosi, in 1931.   5 Ice-cream
vending.   6 *The Jazz Singer*.   7 Franz Liszt.
8 *Pinocchio*.   9 *It Happened One Night* (with Clark Gable
and Claudette Colbert, directed by Frank Capra).
10 *Springtime for Hitler*.   11 Marcello Mastroianni.
12 20th Century-Fox.

**Game 4**   Literature
1 Puck had turned Bottom's head into an ass's head.
2 Sir John Moore.   3 *The Red Badge of Courage*.
4 *Cyrano de Bergerac*.   5 The Duke of Buckingham.
6 *Alice's Adventures In Wonderland* and *Through the
Looking Glass*.   7 The Nightingale (*Ode to a Nightingale*,
John Keats).   8 As a gipsy fortune-teller.   9 A for
Adulteress.   10 Walter Mitty.   11 Becky Sharp.
12 Christian (*The Pilgrim's Progress*).

**Game 4**   The 1970s
1 John Curry.   2 The FIDE world chess championship,
between Bobby Fischer (USA) and Boris Spassky
(USSR).   3 *Rocky*.   4 Mentmore Towers.   5 Lord Louis
Mountbatten.   6 Abba.   7 Spiro Agnew.   8 Victor.
9 Sebastian Coe.   10 Paul Simon.   11 Kent State
University.   12 The United Kingdom's membership of
the EEC.

**Game 4**   Geography
1 Hungary.   2 Vanuatu.   3 The Oder and the Neisse.
4 The Bridge of Sighs.   5 North Korea and South Korea.
6 Hispaniola.   7 Ayers Rock.   8 The Seychelles.
9 Gorky.   10 Denmark.   11 Steep gradient (1 in 7, or
greater).   12 Lebanon.

**Game 4**  Sport
1 Sebastian Coe (Moscow 1980; Los Angeles 1984).
2 Jesse Owens.   3 Swimming (*Fédération Internationale
de Natation Amateur*).    4 Archery (men compete over 90,
70, 50 and 30m; women compete over 70, 60, 50 and
30m).   5 Goal shooter and goal attack.   6 Mark
Thatcher.   7 K.   8 Teleprompter.   9 Real tennis.
10 Argentina.   11 Mike Hawthorne.   12 Lake Placid, USA.

**Game 4**  General Knowledge 2
1 Saint Michael.   2 The coypu.   3 Channel Islands.
4 The Salvation Army.   5 The Berlin airlift.   6 Frederick I.
7 Aeschylus (in 456 BC).   8 In a morris dance troupe (they
are traditional figures which the dancers represent).
9 Two.   10 1936.   11 They both have separate bell towers
or campaniles.   12 A washerman.

**Game 5**  General Knowledge 1
1 Mickey Finn.   2 The Gunpowder Plot of 1605 (they were
fellow conspirators of Guy Fawkes).   3 Irving Berlin.
4 Only the torso is allowed in foil, but the whole body is the
target in épée.   5 The Tomb of Mausolus (Mausoleum).
6 Captain Scarlet.   7 Sophie Tucker.   8 Riser.
9 Woodstock.   10 Ancient lights.   11 It reduces.
12 The Household Cavalry.

**Game 5**  Television
1 Joe Maplin.   2 On *The Streets of San Francisco*.   3 A
rat (Manuel was convinced it was a hamster).   4 Geoffrey
Wheeler (not Jimmy Tarbuck).   5 Bernie the Bolt.
6 Major Harry Kitchener Wellington Truscott (Queen's Own
West Mercian Lowlanders, Retired).   7 *Highway
Patrol*.   8 Crabtree.   9 *Come Dancing* (began 29
September 1950).   10 Bodie.   11 Librarian.   12 Mobile
army surgical hospital.

**Game 5**  Classical Music
1 Leonora (Leonore).   2 Vaughan Williams (known as his
London symphony).   3 *Porgy and Bess* (1955).
4 Moussorgsky's *Pictures at an Exhibition*.   5 Peter
Warlock.   6 Paganini.   7 *Nabucco*.   8 Delius.   9 *The
Beggar's Opera*.   10 Odette.   11 *Samson and
Delilah*.   12 Joke.

**Game 5** Transport
1 Tachograph.  2 R101.  3 The Morris Minor.  4 Lyons
(TGV stands for *train grande Vitesse*).  5 The *Great
Britain*.  6 In a flying accident.  7 BOAC.  8 Jaguar.
9 The escalator (at Earls Court Underground station).
10 The Ford Model T.  11 Great Western Railway (GWR).
12 The Schneider Trophy.

**Game 5** Pop Music
1 Jimmy Somerville, their lead singer.  2 *Misty*.  3 The
Bee Gees.  4 *Merry Christmas Everybody*.  5 *Lily the
Pink* (The Scaffold).  6 Lionel Richie.  7 Billy Joe
McAllister.  8 Yazoo.  9 The Who.  10 'Another day older
and deeper in debt'.  11 *Bad Moon Rising*.  12 The
Boomtown Rats.

**Game 5** Food and Drink
1 Dr Johnson.  2 It consists of raw fish.  3 Sally Lunn.
4 Pasteurisation of milk.  5 United States of America (not
China).  6 Gorgonzola.  7 Waldorf salad.  8 Sprinkling
with flour or other powder.  9 Fermented mare's milk.
10 South or Central America (tropical America).  11 A mild
infusion of herbs or flowers – herb tea.  12 Firm to the
teeth.

**Game 5** Living World
1 Octopus.  2 Gannet.  3 Rookery.  4 Swim bladder.
5 Pansy.  6 Whale shark.  7 Hippopotamus.  8 Borzoi.
9 Gizzard (a muscular section of the stomach).
10 Newt.  11 Green.  12 Leatherjacket.

**Game 5** General Knowledge (2)
1 One to six.  2 *Jaws*.  3 Kow tow.  4 Euclid.  5 GDAE.
6 Greece.  7 Winston Churchill.  8 Dar-Es-Salaam.
9 Joan of Arc.  10 Polio.  11 Sulphuric acid.  12 Lincoln.

**Game 6** General Knowledge (1)
1 Dr Crippen.  2 Jehovah's Witnesses.  3 Yorick
(*Hamlet*).  4 M 90.  5 Gunpowder.  6 The Jam.  7 Two
weeks (no different from anywhere else in Scotland).
8 Malawi.  9 Mercury.  10 Brighton.  11 Old
Hundredth.  12 Friends and acquaintances.

**Game 6**   Cinema
1 Sonny (Santino).   2 *Snow White and the Seven Dwarfs*.   3 *Billy Liar*.   4 *Ryan's Daughter*.   5 Richard Gere.   6 The Bowery Boys.   7 *Khartoum*.   8 1924 (in Paris).   9 Rooster Cogburn (in *True Grit*, 1969).   10 Joan Crawford.   11 *Vertigo*.   12 *Day for Night*.

**Game 6**   Sport
1 Gary Lineker and Peter Beardsley.   2 Six.   3 Forwards and backs.   4 Billy Wright.   5 Table tennis.   6 Mary Dekker Slaney (who won in 4 minutes 16.71 seconds).   7 Arsenal.   8 England.   9 Olga Korbut.   10 Gerrie Coetzee (South Africa).   11 Lacrosse.   12 501.

**Game 6**   History
1 The Gordon Riots.   2 The Ku Klux Klan.   3 The Ottoman Empire.   4 Perkin Warbeck.   5 The water closet.   6 They were three of the victims of Jack the Ripper.   7 Mary, Queen of Scots (the victim was David Rizzio, 1566).
8 Tokyo Rose.   9 The island of Heligoland.
10 Mayerling.   11 The Black and Tans.   12 Peary.

**Game 6**   Food and Drink
1 Vine leaves.   2 Ratatouille.   3 Bourbon whisky.
4 Salami.   5 Mexico (it is a state and a town).   6 Baking powder.   7 Duchesse potatoes.   8 Ambrosia.
9 Avocado.   10 Brandy and Cointreau.   11 Barley.
12 Parmesan or Gruyère.

**Game 6**   Television
1 James Clavell.   2 John Forsythe.   3 *Cathy Come Home*.   4 Silver.   5 *Till Death Us Do Part*.   6 *Mind Your Language*.   7 The Krankies.   8 *Lovejoy*.   9 Brother and sister (twins).   10 *Crackerjack*.   11 Edith.   12 Leslie Mitchell.

## Game 6  Literature
1 John Betjeman (*Slough*).   2 Fortinbras.   3 Ghent and Aix (*How They Brought The Good News From Ghent to Aix*).   4 *The Admirable Crichton*.   5 Dorian Gray (*The Picture of Dorian Gray*).   6 *Zuleika Dobson*.   7 *Anna Karenina*.   8 *Amadeus*.   9 Madame Defarge.   10 Joseph Conrad.   11 Percy Bysshe Shelley.   12 Catherine Earnshaw.

## Game 6  General Knowledge (2)
1 'We'll keep the red flag flying here'.   2 Advanced gas-cooled reactor.   3 *The Midwich Cuckoos*.   4 Trotsky.   5 Daedalus.   6 Belgium.   7 Nipper.   8 Dan Archer.   9 L. Ron Hubbard.   10 Jeremy Bentham.   11 *Hey Jude*.   12 The supporter.

## Game 7  General Knowledge (1)
1 Poet Laureate.   2 The wearing of seat belts for drivers and front seat passengers in motor cars.   3 Morgan le Fay.   4 Twenty-eight.   5 The drinking of the loyal toast.   6 The Matterhorn.   7 Captain W. E. Johns.   8 Chiang Ching.   9 100.   10 Helium.   11 The Royal Company of Archers.   12 The Knights of Columbus.

## Game 7  History
1 The First Crusade.   2 Ramsay MacDonald (in 1924).   3 The French Protestants, or Huguenots.   4 Oliver Cromwell.   5 The striking miners.   6 The Marquess of Queensbury.   7 British ambassador to Naples (British envoy).   8 A sword.   9 Anders Celsius.   10 Dick Whittington.   11 Abraham Lincoln (in Ford's Theatre, Washington).   12 Montezuma.

## Game 7  Pop Music
1 Alexei Sayle.   2 Eric Clapton.   3 *Angel Face*.   4 *YMCA*.   5 The Young Ones.   6 His socks (they glow).   7 Fiddler's Dram.   8 Stevie Wonder.   9 'Just slip out the back Jack'.   10 1969.   11 Bob Marley (Robert Nesta Marley).   12 *House of the Rising Sun*.

**Game 7** Living World
1 64in.   2 Chlorophyll.   3 Common lizard.   4 Endangered or threatened species.   5 Thirteen (plus a head).
6 (Reef-building) coral.   7 Compound eye.   8 Coypu.
9 Zebra.   10 Plaice.   11 Marsupium.   12 Wolverine.

**Game 7** Cinema.
1 *Superman*.   2 Charlie Chaplin.   3 William Hanna and Joseph Barbera.   4 *The Lady Vanishes*.   5 Vienna.
6 *Exodus*.   7 *Westworld*.   8 *Macbeth*.   9 Mary Astor (playing the part of Brigid O'Shaughnessy).   10 *Destry Rides Again*.   11 *I'm All Right Jack*.   12 Mack Sennett.

**Game 7** The 1960s
1 Cigarette advertisements.   2 'Ginger' Marks.   3 The Joy Strings.   4 Tristan da Cunha.   5 Dr Emile Savundra.
6 Alexander Dubcek.   7 They rowed across the Atlantic (in *English Rose III*).   8 Sir Seretse Khama.   9 The Tet offensive.   10 Prince Juan Carlos (of Spain).
11 The Berlin Wall.   12 Alcatraz.

**Game 7** Geography
1 Brown Willy.   2 South India.   3 Libya.
4 Fermanagh.   5 Newmarket.   6 South Africa.   7 It is a whirlpool.   8 Afghanistan and Pakistan.   9 Guernsey.
10 French.   11 Czechoslovakia.   12 Chile.

**Game 7** General Knowledge 2
1 River Thames.   2 Anwar Sadat.   3 Maundy Thursday.   4 The Turkey.   5 Michael Caine.   6 Rapid eye movement.   7 His spring cleaning.   8 After Janus, the Roman god who was two-faced (looking forward and looking back).   9 Council for the Protection of Rural England.   10 Amy Johnson.   11 Harry Lauder.   12 Eight.

**Game 8** General Knowledge 1
1 *Achille Lauro*.   2 Mary (the mother of Jesus).   3 Charles de Gaulle.   4 Jacob, his twin brother.   5 'Duke' Ellington.   6 Sixteen.   7 The papal Swiss Guards.
8 Cana.   9 10/6d.   10 Victor Hugo.   11 Sarah Brightman.   12 Backgammon.

**Game 8** Sport
1 He found the World Cup. (Pickles was the dog who
discovered the cup under a hedge a week after it had been
stolen.)   2 A throw in wrestling.   3 Cricket stumps.
4 The Greyhound Derby (Mick the Miller, 1929 and 1930;
Patricia's Hope, 1972 and 1973).   5 The Derby.   6 Mark
Spitz (swimmer).   7 Stones or granites.   8 Cassius Clay
(later Muhammad Ali).   9 Terry Griffiths.   10 Sarah
Hardcastle.   11 The National Stud.   12 Alain Prost (1985
and 1986).

**Game 8** Literature
1 *Gulliver's Travels*.   2 *Volpone*.   3 *Richard III*.   4 *The
Moonstone*.   5 The Prioress, Madame Eglantyne.
6 Nevil Shute.   7 *For Whom the Bell Tolls*.   8 C. S.
Forester.   9 Eliza Doolittle.   10 *Utopia*.   11 Injun
Joe.   12 One whose name is the title of a work: eg *Oliver
Twist*.

**Game 8** Television
1 Mrs Cadogan.   2 *King of the Ghetto*.   3 They are
cousins.   4 *All In Good Faith*.   5 He had six.   6 Rose (the
maid).   7 Huw Wheldon.   8 She was electrocuted by a
hair-dryer.   9 *Callan*.   10 *The Great Egg Race*.   11 *The
Beverly Hillbillies*.   12 *The Incredible Hulk* (Bill Bixby plays
David Banner, Lou Ferrigno plays the Incredible Hulk).

**Game 8** Food and Drink
1 Pesto.   2 India.   3 Cold, iced or chilled.   4 Fry in oil or
fat in a covered pan.   5 A type of bread.   6 Rioja.
7 Coffee.   8 Hazel.   9 Pig's head (occasionally sheep or
cow heads).   10 Terrine.   11 Parboil.   12 Seaweed.

**Game 8** The 1960s
1 Jim Clark (1962, 1963, 1964, 1965, 1967).   2 Algeria
(1965).   3 1964 (10 March).   4 Identikit.   5 Coco the
Clown.   6 Betting shops.   7 Leatherslade Farm.
8 Malcolm X.   9 Blue Streak.   10 Dr Ramsey.   11 In
Place of Strife.   12 Mr Harold Holt.

**Game 8   Classical Music**
1 *Coppelia*.   2 *No 8 in B minor*.   3 Gilbert.
4 *Messiah*.   5 Double bass.   6 Emperor.   7 *Air on a
G-string*.   8 *Cinderella*.   9 *Karelia*.   10 The Philadelphia
Orchestra.   11 *The Dream of Gerontius*.   12 Hoffmann
(the poet in *Tales of Hoffmann*).

**Game 8   General Knowledge (2)**
1 3 no trump.   2 The House of Lords.
3 Hispano-Suiza.   4 It consists entirely of silence.
5 Gauleiter.   6 Halberd or partizan.   7 Portugal.
8 Embracery.   9 Papyrus reed.   10 Helen Keller.
11 Parallax.   12 Minimum speed 30 mph.

**Game 9   General Knowledge (1)**
1 It does not have one (first amendment to the
constitution, 1791).   2 Billy Paul.   3 Cromarty Firth.
4 Lord Delfont   5 First lieutenant.   6 Sulphuric acid.
7 Mars and Jupiter.   8 Melbourne.   9 Brian.   10 Davy
Crockett.   11 The Lapps.   12 Whisky, or Irish Whiskey.

**Game 9   Living World**
1 Vegetable.   2 Kodiak (or Alaskan) brown bear.
3 Common or Greek tortoise (spur-thighed tortoise).
4 Red jungle fowl.   5 Hexagonal (six-sided).   6 Tsetse fly.
7 Insectivora.   8 Three-toed sloth or ai.   9 North
America.   10 Fish.   11 Cane.   12 Bandicoot.

**Game 9   Geography**
1 Carrara.   2 Madison Avenue.   3 A village, town or
settlement.   4 Sicily.   5 The Norfolk Broads.   6 New
Zealand (South Island).   7 Laos.   8 Belgium.   9 The Mull
of Kintyre.   10 Fiji.   11 The Roaring Forties.
12 Sheerness.

**Game 9   Cinema**
1 Mickey Rooney.   2 *The Jewel of the Nile*.   3 Monument
Valley.   4 *The African Queen* (played by Bogart).
5 Johnny Mercer.   6 Spencer Tracy and Katharine
Hepburn.   7 Bates Motel.   8 *Love Me Tender*.
9 *Star!*   10 Lionel Jeffries.   11 Betty Hutton.
12 *West Side Story*.

**Game 9   History**
1 Sir Ernest Shackleton.   2 Lady Godiva.   3 Thomas Torquemada.   4 Pitcairn.   5 York (known as Yarvik to the Vikings).   6 The Iceni.   7 Saladin.   8 Scurvy.   9 The Mensheviks.   10 Disraeli.   11 Wessex.   12 Portugal.

**Game 9   Television**
1 Martin.   2 The Department of Administrative Affairs.
3 *The Young Ones*.   4 Robert McKenzie.   5 *Steptoe and Son*.   6 *Shine on Harvey Moon*.   7 Sophia.   8 Eliot Ness.   9 Tannochbrae.   10 *Quincy*.   11 *Death of a Princess*.   12 Alfred Hitchcock (*Alfred Hitchcock Presents*).

**Game 9   Food and Drink**
1 The air gap between the cork and the wine.   2 Pumpkin pie.   3 Russia.   4 Chicory.   5 Beaujolais (the *Beaujolais nouveau* race).   6 Ground almonds and sugar.
7 Australia.   8 Cheese.   9 Scallops.   10 Puff pastry.
11 Brandy and Benedictine.   12 Herring.

**Game 9   General Knowledge (2)**
1 Three (Christmas past, present and future).
2 Eisenhower.   3 A style of bricklaying – with headers (ends of bricks) and stretchers (sides) showing alternately.
4 Soda water.   5 Tara.   6 Borstal.   7 A quadrant.
8 Sean O'Casey.   9 Copenhagen.   10 Jules Léotard.
11 Peninsular and Oriental.   12 Hinduism. It is one of the manifestations of Vishnu.

**Game 10   General Knowledge (1)**
1 Damon Runyon.   2 Tatum O'Neal.   3 Capricorn.
4 Patty Hearst.   5 *Show Boat*.   6 20.00 hours (8 pm).
7 Eskimo.   8 Silver Ghost.   9 Martin Luther King.
10 Women's javelin.   11 Supreme Headquarters Allied Powers Europe.   12 Stocking stitch.

**Game 10    Literature**
1 James Joyce.   2 Dylan Thomas.   3 *Blithe Spirit.*
4 Antonio.   5 Edgar Allen Poe (*The Murders in the Rue Morgue*).   6 *Divina Commedia – The Divine Comedy.*
7 Young Jolyon (Forsyte).   8 Ayesha.   9 Horace Rumpole.   10 Fanny goes to the wrong church.   11 *The Duchess of Malfi.*   12 *Lady Chatterley's Lover.*

**Game 10    Cinema**
1 *ET.*   2 *The Enforcer.*   3 *Bad Day at Black Rock.*   4 *Torn Curtain.*   5 Basil Rathbone.   6 *The Alamo.*   7 Daniel Day Lewis.   8 Abbott and Costello.   9 Greta Garbo (in *Anna Christie*, 1930).   10 Sylvester Stallone.   11 Buck Barrow (Clyde's brother).   12 *The Shining.*

**Game 10    Pop Music**
1 It Bites.   2 Kris Kristofferson.   3 Paul McCartney.
4 *Xanadu.*   5 UB40.   6 The death of John Bonham (their drummer).   7 Venus.   8 *Blue Suede Shoes.*   9 The Clash.   10 Dexy's Midnight Runners.   11 Maddie Prior.   12 Bananarama.

**Game 10    The 1960s**
1 The *Daily Herald.*   2 Aberdeen.   3 Stephen Ward.
4 Simon Dee.   5 Colonel Gaddafi.   6 Coventry.   7 Alexei Kosygin.   8 *Itchycoo Park.*   9 Foinavon.
10 Greece.   11 British Railways.   12 Louis Washkansky.

**Game 10    Sport**
1 Grundy.   2 *Tour de France.*   3 Karen Barber and Nicky Slater.   4 Angling (it is a salmon fly).   5 Mexico.
6 Jersey Joe Walcott.   7 Sussex.   8 High jumping. (He invented the 'Fosberry flop' technique.)   9 Malcolm Nash.   10 Tic-tac.   11 Badminton.   12 Nigel Mansell.

**Game 10    Geography**
1 The Strait of Messina (between Italy and Sicily).   2 The Saint Lawrence.   3 A small mountain lake.   4 Zagreb.
5 Colombia.   6 Arctic Ocean.   7 Norway and Russia.
8 Berne.   9 Jutland.   10 Lake Titicaca.
11 Mississippi.   12 Fingal's Cave.

**Game 10**   General Knowledge (2)
1 1978 (Paul VI, John Paul I and John Paul II).
2 Robot.   3 Marat.   4 Velázquez.   5 The troposphere.
6 Bombardier.   7 Simon Legree.   8 A musician (you
would be a Licentiate of the Royal Academy of Music).
9 Randolph Turpin.   10 The oak.   11 Remembrance
Sunday.   12 Squab.